A BAKER'S FIELD GUIDE TO
Holiday Candy & Confections

Sweet Treats All Year Long

DEDE WILSON

THE HARVARD COMMON PRESS

Boston, Massachusetts

THE HARVARD COMMON PRESS
535 Albany Street
Boston, Massachusetts 02118
www.harvardcommonpress.com

Copyright © 2005 by Dede Wilson

Printed in China

Printed on acid-free paper

Library of Congress Cataloging-in-Publication Data

Wilson, Dede.
   A baker's field guide to holiday candy & confections : sweet treats all year long / Dede Wilson.
       p. cm.
   Includes index.
   ISBN 1-55832-309-0 (hc : alk. paper)
1. Candy. 2. Confectionery. 3. Holiday cookery.
   4. Cookery, International. I. Title.
   TX791.W59 2005
   641.5'83—dc22

                                                    2005004952

ISBN-13: 978-1-55832-309-4
ISBN-10: 1-55832-309-0

10 9 8 7 6 5 4 3 2 1

Book design by Night & Day Design
Cover and interior photographs © 2005 Eric Roth Photography
Candy and confection preparation and styling by Mary Bandereck

To the women in my life—you enrich

it immeasurably: Julie Angell, Emily

Boudreault, Claudia Brown, Liz Cantor,

Julie Chartier, Marion Dussault,

Barbara Fairchild, Annie Kelly, Kristine

Kidd, Linda Kielson, Maureen Lasher,

Suzanne LoManto, Mary McNamara,

Juanita Plimpton, Marge Poore,

Judy Pozar, Pam Rys, Amara Staffanell

Wagner, Amy Wasserman, Ravenna

Wilson, Belle, Hope . . . and to

Steve Kelly

Contents

Acknowledgments

This book has a large international component and many people helped me track down recipes and traditions. Some are friends and family, some are people whom I enlisted on the spot at IACP (International Association of Culinary Professionals) conventions. . . . Then there are the people I met on planes or at parties, or whom I e-mailed cold. I cannot thank all of you enough, and I am afraid that I will probably leave someone out, so please forgive any oversights.

Thanks to Maria Kijac and Marcela Sorondo for South American candy information; Faye Levy for insights into Jewish cuisine; Anne Marie Aznarez for help in researching Spanish confections; Darra Goldstein for information on Russian sweets; David Lebovitz for his Francophile knowledge; David Jesson from Peru; Enge Berit for her Norwegian recipe—in Norwegian! And thanks to Pam Juengling, who led me to Anne Donnelly, who helped with translation; Raghavan Iyer came to the rescue with Indian recipes, as did Darin Sarin, whom I met on a plane quite fortuitously! Jill Hough from COPIA made phone calls for me to Guatemala; Kim de la Villefromoy from "down unda" introduced me to copha (see page 144); Lily de Jensen came through with information on Colombian candies; and Evie Arharidis and Naomi Waynee, both of whom I know through our beloved yet silly dogs, sent recipes and ideas. Elizabeth Andoh generously spoke with me all the way from Japan; Arzu Yilmaz gave me her Turkish Delight recipe. I have a lot of new friends!

Pam Hoenig, editor extraordinaire, goes to the top of this list. She brought me to The Harvard Common Press, where I found a happy home, and this is our third collaboration. The Field Guide concept was hers, and I feel blessed that she enlisted me to bring it to life. Pam wasn't able to see the book through to the end; the final piece of work was guided beautifully by Valerie Cimino. Thank you to Debra Hudak for copyediting help. The folks at The Harvard Common Press keep the pages turning, so to speak: Bruce Shaw, publisher; Jodi Marchowsky, production editor; Virginia Downes, production manager; Christine Corcoran Cox, managing editor; Pat Jalbert-Levine, project manager; Skye Stewart, publicity director; Betsy Young, sales director; Liza Beth, publicist; Julie Strane, special sales manager; Amy

Etcheson, marketing assistant; and Megan Weireter, office manager. Heartfelt thanks to my agents, Maureen and Eric Lasher, who feel more like extended family.

Thank you to Jered Thorp and Wilton for helping with equipment and supplies. Thanks to Mary McNamara, the best baking and cooking buddy I could ask for.

Thanks to David Kilroy, my partner—he'd prefer to help me test a book on tofu, but he puts up with the sugar and chocolate.

And finally, thank you to my kids, Freeman, Forrester, and Ravenna, who help test whatever I'm working on—and always have helpful suggestions.

Introduction

Candy might not be the first thing you think about making when you head for the kitchen. Cookies are easy, cakes are whipped up for birthdays, but candy? Perhaps many of us think about candy as something we grab on the go—as in a chocolate bar midafternoon—or, more often, as a special treat for a special occasion: multicolored candy canes at Christmas, hollow and solid chocolate Easter bunnies, and saltwater taffy and fudge from a seaside general store. The fact is that many candies from around the world are easy and fun to make at home with readily available ingredients—and any homemade candy is sure to impress.

The holiday candy tradition spans the globe, and I have gathered together candies and confections from all over the world for you to enjoy during your next special occasion, be it Easter, Valentine's Day, Purim, or the Day of the Dead. Some of the candies are traditional, like the Glazed Chestnuts from France (page 146) or the Egg Yolk Nougat (Turron de Yema) from Spain (page 156). Others were created just for you, like the Champagne and Cherry Heart Lollipops on page 46.

So, stock up on the sugar—let's make candy!

How to Use This Book

This is the third Baker's Field Guide, accompanying *A Baker's Field Guide to Christmas Cookies* and *A Baker's Field Guide to Chocolate Chip Cookies*.

This user-friendly format gives each candy its own two-page spread, where you will find the Holiday it is associated with, the Type (such as hand-formed candy, bar candy, or molded candy), its Habitat (country of origin), a Description (what you can expect to taste), Field Notes (where I give you tips and background information), any Related Species (variations), and a Lifespan (that gives storage information and how long you can expect the candy to stay fresh). At the end of many recipes is a Candy Tidbit (where you will find resource information, as well as anything important about the candy that I thought would be helpful to you). For each candy you will also find symbols for special characteristics, as listed in the following chart:

Ingredients

Here is a short list of frequently called for ingredients used in this book. If you start with high-quality ingredients, you'll get the best results.

BUTTER: Use fresh unsalted butter.

GRANULATED SUGAR: Use regular white granulated sugar.

Superfine sugar: Superfine sugar is available nationwide from Domino. It is sometimes referred to as bar sugar because bartenders use it for its ability to dissolve quickly.

Light and dark brown sugar: These should be packed into a measuring cup when measuring.

Confectioners' sugar: Also called powdered sugar, this almost always needs sifting before using.

Colored sugars: Colored sugars are used to decorate candies and can be found in a variety of hues. See Resources for ordering information.

HONEY AND MOLASSES: Use mild-flavored orange blossom or wildflower honey and unsulfured molasses for these candies. Lightly coat the inside of your liquid measuring cup with nonstick cooking spray, then pour in the desired amount. It will then slip right out.

EGGS: Use eggs graded "large."

FLOUR: Use all-purpose flour. These recipes were tested with King Arthur Unbleached All-Purpose Flour.

LEAVENERS: Make sure your baking soda is fresh.

SALT: Use regular table salt for these candies; coarse salts measure differently.

MILK, CREAM CHEESE, AND SOUR CREAM: Use full-fat varieties.

HEAVY CREAM: For best results, use cream labeled "heavy" as opposed to "whipping." The "heavy" has a higher butterfat content.

EXTRACTS: Use pure vanilla, almond, and mint extracts.

FLAVORINGS: Candy flavorings, such as cherry or mint, can vary widely in strength and quality. For best results, use the brands I suggest in the individual recipes, as that is how they were tested.

CITRUS OILS: Boyajian makes amazing orange, lemon, lime, grapefruit, and tangerine oils. Extracts cannot be substituted. See Resources for ordering information.

CITRUS ZESTS: Use only the colored part of the zest, not the bitter white pith underneath.

CHOCOLATE: Most candies that contain chocolate feature chocolate as the dominant flavor, so it is vitally important to use the best-quality chocolate that you can obtain. Many high-quality chocolates can be found in specialty food stores, or try one of the numerous mail-order sources.

Bittersweet and semisweet chocolate: While these chocolates can be used interchangeably with fairly reliable results, if I specify a particular type of chocolate, I suggest using it for best results. I often use Scharffen Berger and Valrhona chocolates for candy making.

Milk chocolate: Use high-quality brands such as Michel Cluizel, Callebaut, and Valrhona.

White chocolate: Look for white chocolate that lists cocoa butter in the ingredients rather than palm oil or other oils. The cocoa butter will give it a natural chocolate flavor and aroma. I most often use Callebaut and Valrhona.

Couverture chocolate: This is chocolate that has a cocoa butter content of at least 32 percent. It will be very fluid in nature when melted, and it gives molded chocolates or coated chocolates and candies the thinnest, most elegant coating.

Chocolate coating or confectionery coating: This is a chocolate-like product that comes in white, milk, and dark varieties, but it does not contain any cocoa butter. Its fat content comes from various oils instead. It does not have the rich flavor of high-quality chocolate made with cocoa butter, but it is very easy to melt and use, does not need to be tempered, and has practical uses in child-friendly confections.

COCOA: These recipes call for unsweetened Dutch-processed cocoa powder as well as natural cocoa powder, so check the label. For Dutch-processed, it might say "Dutch," "Dutched," or "alkalized," but if it says "natural," that's the other kind. You can find both in the supermarket.

NUTS: Make sure nuts are fresh, with no rancid smell.

COCONUT: The type required will be specified in the individual recipe. Unsweetened desiccated coconut is finely grated in texture, and it can be found in natural foods stores. Sweetened flaked coconut is made up of larger shreds and can be found in the supermarket, usually alongside the chocolate morsels.

SPICES: All of the spices called for in this book are ground; please make sure they are fresh.

CANDIED FRUIT PEELS: Buy high-quality candied fruit peels at a specialty or gourmet store, or see Resources for ordering information.

GOLD AND SILVER LEAF: You can buy these at art supply stores, or see Resources for ordering information. Just be sure to buy at least 22-karat gold and pure silver with no aluminum or other metals for them to be safe enough to use with food.

Equipment

THERMOMETER: You will need an accurate candy thermometer for these recipes. You can buy inexpensive glass thermometers in the supermarket, and they do work, but they can be hard to read, can break easily, and may not allow you to read a degree-by-degree increase in temperature, which I find helpful (they often go by five-degree increments). Like any kitchen tool, the better the design, the more you will get out of it, and the right thermometer can make the difference between enjoying candy making and having a frustrating experience. I absolutely love the Redi Chek digital thermometer made by Maverick. See Resources for ordering information.

MEASURING CUPS AND SPOONS: For dry ingredients, I use high-quality stainless-steel cups that are sturdy enough not to dent (dents make for inaccurate measurements). The same goes for measuring spoons. For liquid measurements, I use the standard Pyrex measuring cups available at most supermarkets and kitchenware stores.

MIXER: I used a freestanding 5-quart KitchenAid mixer to test these recipes. If using a handheld mixer, the mixing times will be longer.

FOOD PROCESSOR: The recipes were tested using a KitchenAid 11-cup Ultra Power Food Processor. You will need a food processor with a metal blade to make these recipes.

MICROWAVE OVEN: It is hard to standardize recipes using microwave ovens, as each model's wattage varies. Always follow your manufacturer's directions for specific information. I use the microwave to melt dark chocolate and butter. Start by microwaving on 30 percent power for short periods of time.

JELLY-ROLL PANS: These recipes were tested with heavyweight aluminum or stainless-steel rimmed pans (sometimes referred to as half-sheet pans or sheet pans). You will be using these pans for poured candies and barks, as well as to provide a flat surface for supporting some candies, such as the Christmas Divinity on page 136. Therefore, it is very important that your jelly-roll pans are flat and free of dents and nicks.

ALUMINUM FOIL: Many recipes call for a smooth surface of aluminum foil on which to form the candies. I absolutely love Reynolds' new Release aluminum foil, which has a nonstick surface and is perfect for candy making. If you can't find it, regular aluminum foil with a spritz of nonstick cooking spray will work just fine.

PARCHMENT PAPER: Parchment is available in rolls, like aluminum foil, from kitchenware stores and supermarkets.

WAXED PAPER: This can be used to separate layers of candies during storage. However, I find parchment paper to be so much more versatile. You may use either.

ACETATE: This is clear plastic that comes in rolls or sheets, and you can buy it at an art-supply store. It is used in a fashion similar to parchment paper in that it provides a nonstick surface, but it also gives a nice high sheen to the surface of some chocolates, such as any of the dipped truffles. (Do not use it in the oven.)

PASTRY BAG, COUPLER, AND TIPS: Pastry bags with decorating tips are used to pipe out certain candies or to add decorative elements to others. I like the Feather-weight bags made by Wilton, as they are soft and flexible. A coupler is a plastic attachment that fits into the bag and allows you to change tips easily.

MICROPLANE GRATER: When you need citrus zest, reach for a microplane grater. They are extremely sharp, precise tools that will grate the colored peel right off of any fruit while leaving all the bitter white pith behind.

CHOCOLATE DIPPING TOOLS: Some truffles and chocolates are dipped into melted chocolate. You can use your fingers or two forks to toss the candies back and forth until coated. However, there are specific dipping tools that work very well. There are a few different shapes; one looks like a loop that can cradle a round candy, such as a truffle. The others are different variations of forks. They usually come in a set. Wilton makes some inex-pensive ones that are worth trying even if you only make candy occasionally.

CANDY WRAPPERS: Some candies, such as taffy, should be stored individually wrapped. You can certainly cut up little 4-inch or 5-inch squares of parchment paper, but you can also buy all sorts of pretty, inexpensive papers designed just for this purpose. They come in clear cellophane, metallic foils, and varied colored papers and can be purchased wherever candy-making ingredients and tools are sold (see Resources for ordering information).

BENCH SCRAPER: This is a rectangular piece of stainless steel with a wooden or hard plastic handle along one long side. I use it to gather ingredients together from my work surface, scrape up bits of dry ingredients, like chopped chocolate, spread fudge into pans, and scrape my work surface clean. But my favorite use is for cutting brownies and bars cleanly, so it occurred to me that one could be used for cutting soft candies such as fudge, Turkish Delight, and any other candies that are in a pan and need to be sectioned (see page 14, Recipe Yields and Cutting Candy).

CANDY MOLDS: If you make candy on a regular basis, you likely already own some candy molds. But otherwise, you probably do not own any—yet! In this book I use plastic molds and silicone molds (see Resources for purchasing infor-mation). There are metal molds available, but they scratch easily and are harder to maintain. There are various types that I would like to introduce you to:

3-D molds for solid molding: These are the type of molds used for the Solid

Chocolate Bunnies on page 66 and can be used for the Good Luck Marzipan Pig on page 26. These molds have two halves that mirror one another. They are usually made from very heavy plastic or metal (but again, plastic is preferred). Some expensive ones have extremely strong magnets that hold the two halves together, and these make gorgeous candies with hardly any seams. Most come with metal clips that hold them together. They sometimes come with open bottoms into which you pour the chocolate, but they might not, as these molds are also used for hollow molding or different kinds of solid molding, such as for the marzipan pig. Ask the vendor when purchasing, as many molds can have their bottoms cut out for you before delivery. Some will be built so that they can be propped up by themselves. Others need to be supported after they are filled with chocolate. Again, describe what you want to do and the vendor can help you accomplish the task.

Flat-backed molds: These are also used for solid molding. They look like half of a 3-D mold and are easy to use. Tempered chocolate is simply poured into the mold up to the rim, which is the back of the mold. After the chocolate has firmed and hardened, the shape is unmolded and flipped over. Any details will be on the opposite side, and the candy will rest on its flat surface.

Molds for hollow molding: Some 3-D molds can be used for hollow molding. Others are specifically made for this purpose and will not have an opening in the bottom. The Easter Egg with a Surprise on page 70 uses a mold made for the purpose of hollow molding. I will show you how to fill, then empty, the two halves so that they can be sealed together to yield a hollow chocolate candy.

When purchasing a mold, look for several features:

- **Detail:** The more detailed the mold, the more detailed your candies will be. This is important when it comes to items such as chocolate rabbits, where details such as fur texture and eye shape are important. If the mold is smooth and rounded, as with an egg, then the candy surface will be completely smooth.

- **Weight:** Clear plastic molds come in different weights of plastic, which are commonly referred to as either hobby grade, which is lighter, or professional grade, which is heavier and stiffer, although still flexible. The heavier choice is usually better. Not only will a heavier mold withstand the rigors of time better, but also any detail is likely to be more deeply etched and precise. Both grades are inexpensive.

- **Plaques and cavities:** These are not dental terms! A plaque is a mold that holds several candy designs on one

Tempering Chocolate for Dipping

Some of the candies in the book call for a dip in chocolate. If the chocolate is tempered, which simply means melting it in a particular way, the results will be very professional looking. This is accomplished by a precise melting procedure, which stabilizes the fat crystals in the cocoa butter and prevents the chocolate from streaking after cooling. Tempered chocolate will stay glossy even without refrigeration and add a polished look to your candies. When it comes to molded candies, such as the Rainbow Chocolate Fish and the Easter Egg with a Surprise, the chocolate must be tempered in order for it to behave properly within the mold. Aside from the aesthetic attributes, tempered chocolate will set quickly and contract upon cooling, which make the molding process much more successful.

To temper chocolate:
- Start with desired amount of chocolate as stated in recipe and chop it very finely.
- Place about two-thirds of it in the top of a double boiler set over gently simmering water.
- Stir gently to encourage melting, but not vigorously, which will add air.
- Do not allow chocolate to heat above 115°F for semisweet or bittersweet chocolate and 110°F for milk or white chocolate. As soon as the chocolate is melted, remove it from the heat and wipe the bottom of the pot to eliminate any chances of water droplets reaching the chocolate, which would cause it to seize. (You'll know if it has seized because it will become overly thickened and grainy.)
- Add about one-third of the remaining chopped chocolate and stir gently. The

piece of plastic. The plaque is the whole piece. The cavities are the molds themselves, the several impressions made in the plaque. So, for instance, you might have one plaque of fish molds that holds 10 cavities (that is, 10 fish).

- **Number of cavities and yield of recipe:** A recipe might say "Yield: 26 fish," which means that if you want to make the fish all at once, you will need 26 cavities in which to pour the tempered chocolate. You might not want to invest in that

many plaques! So please realize that you must use the recipe yield to help you determine how many plaques to purchase and/or how you will proceed with the recipe if you have fewer cavities than needed.

Recipe Yields and Cutting Candy

Each recipe has a yield number, which tells you how many individual candies or bars (such as fudge) you will get, if you follow my directions. For candies that use molds, I tell you what size mold I use and the yield will say "fifty $1^{1}/_{2}$-inch candies," for instance. If you use different-size molds, the residual heat will melt it, and the mixture will start to cool down.

- Add the remaining chocolate, in two more stages if necessary, to cool the chocolate further, continuing to stir gently until it reaches 79°F. Stir until it is completely melted.
- Place the pot back over hot, but not simmering, water and rewarm the chocolate gently. Semisweet or bittersweet chocolate should be brought up to 88°F; milk or white chocolate should be brought up to 85°F. Do not allow any chocolate to rise above 90°F or you will have to begin the entire process again with the chocolate.

The chocolate is now ready to use. To double-check whether it is ready, thinly spread a teaspoon of the chocolate on a piece of aluminum foil and allow it to cool. The chocolate should look shiny and smooth. Any dull spots or streaks indicate that the chocolate is not in good temper.

Now you must retain the chocolate's temperature while you are working with it. Try setting a heating pad on low and placing your bowl of tempered chocolate on top of it. Always keep checking the temperature, retaining it within its range. Stir it occasionally to keep the entire amount evenly heated, as it will cool around the edges. It will thicken upon cooling, so if it does thicken, it has most likely cooled too much.

Please note that it is easiest to temper at least 8 ounces of chocolate, and it is really not that much more difficult to temper three or four times that amount. If you are making several candies that require tempered chocolate, consider making them on the same day so that you can take advantage of one big batch of tempered chocolate. If you have any leftover tempered chocolate, you can store it at room temperature, wrapped airtight.

recipe might still work, but your yield will be different.

For square or rectangular pieces of candy, the recipe will say "cut into 16 pieces (4 x 4)." This means that you divide the pan into horizontal rows of 4 squares by vertical rows of 4 squares to give you the suggested 16 squares. Squares can often be cut smaller or larger, which will alter your yield. To cut candy such as fudge, I definitely have a preferred method—using a bench scraper (see page 12 for a description of this tool). Take it by the handle and press the sharp edge straight down into the fudge; repeat to make a complete cut either across or down the length of the pan by lifting and pressing, lifting and pressing. If the candy is sticky, wipe the blade clean between cuts with a wet, warm cloth. Cutting in this fashion eliminates the bulk of the drag created by pulling a knife through a pan of candy; the edges will be cleaner and give you prettier results.

Chocolate Tempering Machines

Any retailer or wholesaler that makes their own chocolates will have an industrial-size chocolate temperer that will automatically melt and temper the chocolate, adjusting the temperature as needed. If you make lots of candy that involves tempered chocolate, you might consider buying a home version. The Revolation 1 is the most economical and user-friendly for home use. Chocovision sells the Revolation and has several models from which to choose (see Resources).

Peeling and Toasting Nuts

HAZELNUTS: Spread hazelnuts in a single layer on a sheet pan and bake in a 350°F oven until they begin to give off an aroma and the skins have turned dark brown and have split, exposing the browning nuts. This will take about 10 minutes, depending on amount. Shake the pan once or twice during toasting to encourage even browning. Remove from the oven and cool on a rack, then rub the nuts vigorously between clean kitchen towels until the skins come off. My hazelnuts usually retain a tiny bit of skin on them; that's fine. Hazelnuts can be also purchased already peeled, at an added expense.

ALMONDS: Almonds are sold whole (either blanched or natural), sliced (blanched or natural), and slivered (blanched). Buying whole blanched can save time but costs a bit more. If you want or need to peel whole ones yourself, follow these instructions. Drop them in boiling water and blanch for 1 minute, then drain. Once they're cool enough to handle, you should be able to slip the skins right off with your fingers. To toast almonds, spread them in a single layer on a sheet pan and bake in a 350°F oven until they begin to give off an aroma and

are a light golden brown color. This will take 5 to 10 minutes, depending on the amount of nuts and whether they are whole, slivered, or sliced. Shake the pan once or twice during toasting to encourage even browning. Remove from oven and cool on a rack before using in a recipe.

WALNUTS, PECANS, PISTACHIOS, AND MACADAMIAS: These nuts do not need to be peeled. To toast, follow directions as described above for almonds. The timing will vary depending on the quantity of nuts on the pan, as well as the size of the nut. Always cool nuts before chopping. The oils, which will have been brought to the surface by the heat, must be reabsorbed or the nuts could turn greasy when chopped.

Storing Candies

Candies are extremely varied, from creamy fudge to sugary pralines to lollipops to truffles. I will give you specific storage instructions in each recipe, but generally, most will benefit from being stored in an airtight container, so stock up! They also keep best if stored separately by individual type of candy, so package that fudge separately from those lollies. Some stickier candies, such as the Saltwater Taffy (page 92), will be packaged individually in little candy wrappers, which can be purchased wherever candy-making supplies are sold (see Resources). Certain candies, such as lollipops and hard candies, are best kept absolutely dry and humidity free. There is a product called Blue Magic that helps immensely. It is inexpensive and can be mail ordered (see Resources).

Sending Candies by Mail

Receiving candies through the mail is always a special treat, and it is possible to package your homemade candies in such a way that they arrive in as pristine a condition as when you just made them.

First, choose your candies wisely. Fudge mails well because it is sturdy in shape and density. Individually wrapped candies such as taffy and hard candies mail well too. Truffles can be mailed with a little extra help. Very delicate candies, such as the Spider Webs on page 106, are best enjoyed in your own home! To make this easy for you, in individual recipes I have pointed out with a special icon which candies I think survive the mailing process best.

There are three main categories to consider: individually wrapped candies, candies in fluted paper cups, and chocolates and other candies that require refrigeration.

The simplest candies to mail are those that are individually wrapped, as they may be piled into a tin or airtight container. Since they are each completely wrapped, you may combine candies from different recipes without worrying about their flavors cross-pollinating. If the candies do not fill up the container, place some crumpled plastic wrap on top of the candies, then press the top of the container down onto the plastic wrap. Gently shake the container; the candies should not have any wiggle room. If there is still too much air space and the candies are moving around, add more plastic wrap for cushioning.

For candies in fluted paper cups, begin with a container that has a flat, broad bottom. Nestle the candies, in their cups, side by side, so that they cover the bottom of the container in one even layer. They should fit snugly; you don't want them to slide around. If the container is deep enough you may cover the first layer of candies with parchment paper cut to fit and add a second layer. Even better is a layer of thin, stiff cardboard. This last layer (I don't suggest any more than two layers) should be near the top of the container. Crumple plastic wrap and lay it over the top layer of candies, then press the top of the container down onto the cushioned layer of plastic wrap.

Chocolates and candies that require refrigeration should be packaged in single layers in airtight containers as described previously. In other words, package them close together in single layers, separate the layers with parchment or thin cardboard, and do not make too many layers (again, I prefer a maximum of two). Always cushion the top headspace with crumpled plastic wrap.

Now that you have individual tins and containers filled with candy, they must be placed in a larger shipping container. Place one or more

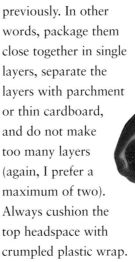

packed containers in a large sturdy box that has been partially filled with Styrofoam "peanuts" packing material, then top off with more peanuts before sealing the box. You want to fill up the outer box with peanuts so that the individual containers are as snug as possible and don't swim around in the box. Alternatively, tape all of the candy containers together, if you are mailing several, then wrap the stack completely with bubble-wrap so that it fits snugly inside your outer box. You can also use crumpled newspaper in lieu of peanuts.

Important: If you are mailing candies that require refrigeration, you must tuck frozen freezer packs here and there inside your outer box. Ideally they will be right next to the containers that hold the candies. In fact, you can tape them to those containers. Cold air sinks, so extra freezer packs can be placed on top of the candy containers and you can label the outside of the box with "This Side Up." I always send these kinds of candies overnight, and in general it is best not to send chocolates in the midsummer months.

Remember that holidays are busy times for the post office. At Christmastime, millions of packages are sent through the mail, so make sure to ask the postmaster how long it will take and plan accordingly. I usually figure extra money into my budget so that I can send my candies overnight or, at the most, two-day post. At the very least, I suggest mailing your packages early in the week to minimize the chances of your candies

sitting in a warehouse over the weekend.

Time vs. Temperature vs. Texture

Recipes often contain visual cues as well as time cues to help you assess doneness. For example: "Bake for about 22 minutes or until golden brown. The sides of the cake should be just pulling away from the sides of the pan." With many candy recipes, however, the temperature is the key cue. There will sometimes be visual cues as well, and where there are helpful ones to give you, I have done so. However, many times you will see a desired temperature listed, such as "cook to 235°F (soft-ball stage)." This is the information you need to determine whether the candy is cooked to the appropriate stage at that point in the recipe or is, in fact, done. For more information on candy temperature ranges and what they mean, and how to make candy without a thermometer, see the chart on page 19. In some recipes you will see that there is no temperature suggested. These are largely recipes that were originally developed without thermometers handy, such as some very old-fashioned recipes or recipes from cultures and/or countries where cooking is approached more intuitively. In these cases, the recipes will suggest cooking times as well as visual or textural cues, as opposed to temperatures.

Ambient Temperature

If you were to visit a professional candy maker, you would see that the air temperatures in the kitchens and work areas are carefully controlled. Candy can be persnickety at times, reacting poorly to heat and humidity. The best-case scenario is to have your kitchen at a cool room temperature, which means around 70°F, and to make candy on a dry day. Air conditioning in the summer is a plus. However, I do not have air conditioning, and I tested all of these recipes during a humid New England summer, so it certainly is possible; it's just not preferable. On a few occasions I had to remake a recipe because it reacted poorly to the heat and humidity, and I don't want you to have to go through the trouble.

American Candy vs. Candies of the World

Americans are known for their immense sugar consumption, but a lot of it is in

Temperature Chart

Stage	Temperature	Description
Thread	230° – 234°F	A small amount dropped into cold water can be picked up, and it will form brittle threads when pulled between your fingertips.
Soft Ball	235° – 240°F	A small ball forms in cold water and feels soft between your fingertips. The ball will feel flexible and flatten when pressed. Fudge, fondants, and pralines are often cooked to this stage.
Firm Ball	242° – 249°F	A small ball forms in cold water and feels firm between your fingertips. The ball will not compress unless pressed quite firmly.
Hard Ball	250° – 265°F	A small ball forms in cold water and feels hard between your fingertips. It can be compressed, but with effort. Nougats, marshmallows, and divinity are often cooked to this stage.
Soft Crack	270° – 290°F	A small amount dropped into cold water will spin into threads. The threads will hold their form out of water but be pliable. Saltwater taffy is often cooked to this stage.
Hard Crack	300° – 310°F	A small amount dropped into cold water will spin into brittle threads. The threads will hold their form out of water and will break if you attempt to bend them. Nut brittles, hard candies, and lollipops are often cooked to this stage.
Caramel	320° – 350°F	Sugar syrup takes on color as it caramelizes. It will first be very pale amber, but it will very quickly turn golden, then deep mahogany. Watch carefully, as the temperature of sugar rises very quickly at this stage.

the form of "hidden" sugars, such as the sweeteners found in condiments, breads, sodas, canned foods, and more. I made an interesting discovery while writing this book: many of the international candies were almost too sweet for my taste! Some of these less familiar candies, such as *Borstplaat,* from Holland, are pure sugar. *Gozinaki,* from Russia, and *Melekouni,* from Greece, are almost pure honey, with some nuts and seeds thrown in for good measure, and they are exceedingly sweet. As you work your way through the recipes, know that some of the candies will be sweet in a way unlike some of their American counterparts. It is not that the recipes are unbalanced; they just represent a different culture's palate. *Vive la différence!*

Precision Is Key

Bakers always say that it is vital to measure accurately and follow instructions precisely in order to get great results. This is even more true with candies. Working with sugar is an art unto itself and requires more attention to detail than any other type of cooking. I implore you to follow these recipes as written to ensure absolutely delicious candies.

Making Candy with Kids

Kids and candy go together. You won't have any trouble convincing kids to *eat* your candy, but I want to address *making* candy with kids. There are many transformations that take place in candy making that kids find fascinating, and the process is educational. However, you will very often be working with high temperatures, and hot sugar, like caramel, can cause severe burns. You can make many of these recipes with kids, but please use your careful judgment about which steps you invite them to help with. For instance, kids might love helping pull sugar and shape candy canes. You, on the other hand, might bring the recipe along to that point by yourself. Youngsters might like to squeeze drops of food coloring into a candy mixture (using their newfound counting skills), while older teenagers might be able to monitor the caramelization of sugar and alert you to when the proper color or temperature is nearing.

How to Make Perfect Candy at Home

- Read every recipe through before starting.
- Use the ingredients called for (for instance, do not substitute salted butter for unsalted).
- Take time to measure accurately with the proper tools (candies often have very few ingredients, so every measurement really counts).
- Use time cues and, when given, visual cues for best results.
- Use temperatures, when given, as precise numbers.
- Store candies according to individual instructions.
- Relax and enjoy the candy-making process!

The
Field Guide

Star-Shaped Marshmallows

▷●◁ **HOLIDAY** *New Year's*

▷●◁ **TYPE** *Poured candy*   ▷●◁ **HABITAT** *United States*

▷●◁ **DESCRIPTION** *These are adorable star- (or snowflake-) shaped marshmallows. They are perfect for kids to have in a cup of hot cocoa on New Year's Eve while the adults are drinking more grown-up beverages.*

▷●◁ **FIELD NOTES** *Maybe you have never thought of making marshmallows at home, but they are actually very easy! The only trick is the timing—you must have the sugar syrup ready at the same time as the egg whites. This is best accomplished by beginning to beat the egg whites about halfway through the sugar syrup's cooking time. A stand mixer is of great help, as you must manage a few steps at one time. Note that you must begin these a day ahead.*

▷●◁ **LIFESPAN** *1 month at room temperature in airtight container in single layers separated by waxed or parchment paper*

Yield: *about 30 stars*

⊳●⊲ INGREDIENTS

¹/₂ cup confectioners' sugar, sifted
¹/₄ cup cornstarch, sifted
¹/₂ cup water
1 tablespoon unflavored gelatin
³/₄ cup plus 2 tablespoons granulated sugar

1 cup light corn syrup
2 large egg whites
¹/₄ teaspoon cream of tartar
2 teaspoons vanilla extract

⊳●⊲ DIRECTIONS

1. Line a jelly-roll pan with aluminum foil, smoothing out any wrinkles. Whisk together confectioners' sugar and cornstarch and sift about half the mixture evenly over the lined pan. Reserve the rest.

2. Stir together ¹/₄ cup of the water and gelatin in a small bowl. Let sit 5 minutes to soften.

3. Meanwhile, stir remaining ¹/₄ cup water, ³/₄ cup sugar, and corn syrup together in a medium-size saucepan.

4. Bring sugar mixture to a simmer over medium heat. At the same time, in a clean, grease-free bowl using an electric mixer at medium speed, beat egg whites until frothy. Add cream of tartar and continue to beat until soft peaks form. As these are beating, check sugar syrup: It should be approaching 240°F (soft-ball stage). Beat 2 tablespoons sugar into egg whites and continue beating until stiff peaks form.

5. When syrup reaches 240°F, remove from heat and whisk in gelatin mixture until it dissolves.

6. When egg whites are ready, slowly add sugar syrup in a thin stream, preventing syrup from hitting the beaters or the sides of the bowl. Beat on high speed until thick, glossy, and cool, about 4 minutes. Beat in vanilla.

7. Scrape mixture onto prepared pan, quickly spreading to a ¹/₂-inch thickness with an offset spatula. Sift remaining sugar-cornstarch mixture over surface. Allow to dry at room temperature overnight. Dip a small, 1¹/₂-inch star-shaped cookie cutter in confectioners' sugar or cornstarch and cut out stars as closely together as possible. Any scraps make great s'mores!

Candy Tidbits

You could flavor these with something other than vanilla if you like. A nice idea is to add a few drops of peppermint extract to the mixture instead. These are great in hot cocoa!

Honey Walnut Candies
(Gozinaki)

>●< **HOLIDAY** *New Year's*

>●< **TYPE** *Poured candy*   >●< **HABITAT** *Russian Georgia*

>●< **DESCRIPTION** *This is a type of nut brittle, featuring mostly honey, with a little bit of sugar as well. Walnuts are traditional, but you could try pecans, if you like. These are sticky and very sweet.*

>●< **FIELD NOTES** *My friends Pam and Jeff Rys have beehives and cultivate honey. There is nothing like raw, unfiltered, unpasteurized honey for its flavor and health benefits, and since I have access to the best, it is what I always use. In candy making, you can get very different results with raw versus processed honey. Therefore, I suggest you use raw, which is readily available in supermarkets. Also, after you chop the nuts, place them in a strainer and shake out and discard any powdery residue. Warning: These are very sticky. The technique of rinsing the wooden board with cold water is often used with very sticky candies. Be patient when you are removing and cutting them; they will come loose eventually.*

>●< **LIFESPAN** *1 week at room temperature in airtight container*

Yield: *30 diamonds*

⋙●⋘ INGREDIENTS

1 cup honey
¹/₄ cup granulated sugar
2 ¹/₄ cups toasted walnut halves, finely
chopped

30 small square candy wrappers or
cellophane

⋙●⋘ DIRECTIONS

1. Rinse a clean, large wooden board with cold water. Allow water droplets to remain on board.

2. Stir honey and sugar together in a large saucepan. Bring to a simmer over medium heat, stirring constantly, until it reaches 220°F; do not burn. Stir in nuts and continue to cook until it reaches 240°F (soft-ball stage) or until golden, which will likely be less than 10 minutes.

3. Scrape mixture onto prepared board. Rinse fingers in cold water and press the mixture out to a flat even layer (about ¹/₂ inch thick); be careful, as candy will be hot.

4. Let candy sit at cool room temperature until cooled and set, about 2 hours.

5. Cut into diamond shapes with a sharp knife dipped in water to help prevent sticking. Pick up individual candies with an offset spatula. Wrap individually in candy wrappers.

Candy Tidbits

Make sure your wooden board
does not smell like onions or your
candy will pick up the flavors! You
could try making these by spreading
the mixture on a rinsed jelly-roll
pan, but I found that the candy
sticks to metal even more
than to wood.

Good Luck Marzipan Pig

🍬 **HOLIDAY** *New Year's, Christmas, birthdays*

🍬 **TYPE** *Molded candy*   🍬 **HABITAT** *Germany*

🍬 **DESCRIPTION** *Marzipan, which is sweetened almond paste, has a strong and distinct flavor that I love. Here the marzipan is simply formed into a pig shape, which is considered to be a lucky image in many cultures. You can use a double-sided 3-D mold or a flat-backed mold or half of a 3-D mold.*

🍬 **FIELD NOTES** *You might wonder what pigs and good luck for the New Year have to do with one another. Well, good-luck images and icons often have to do with health, abundance, and fertility. Pigs certainly are prolific and they tend to be quite healthy and robust. In fact, pigs were symbols of fertility in pre-Judeo-Christian cultures. For best results, use American Almond brand almond paste (see Resources), or look for canned almond paste in the supermarket. Do not use the type sold in a tube, as it does not have the right consistency. A stand mixer is preferable for this very heavy mixture. If you do not have one, simply knead the mixture together with your hands. The powder colors can be found at Beryl's, and the mold I used is from Tomric (see Resources). You could also hand mold the marzipan into a pig shape, if you are so artistically inclined! Note that you have to make the marzipan a day ahead.*

🍬 **LIFESPAN** *1 month at room temperature in airtight container in single layers separated by waxed or parchment paper*

Yield: *3 whole 3-D pigs plus one flat-backed pig, or 7 flat-backed pigs*

Tools: *Tomric pig mold #H-319 (or any pig-shaped mold that is about 5³/₈ inches long x 2¹/₂ inches high)* • *Small soft paintbrush for applying coloring (optional)*

▷●◁ INGREDIENTS

2¹/₂ cups confectioners' sugar, sifted, plus more for sprinkling
1 pound canned almond paste

3 tablespoons light corn syrup
Powder food coloring in colors of your choice (optional)

▷●◁ DIRECTIONS

1. Dust work surface (a clean countertop) with some confectioners' sugar.

2. Crumble almond paste into bowl and add 2¹/₂ cups confectioner's sugar. Beat on low to medium speed with an electric mixer's flat paddle until it has an even, granular appearance. Beat in corn syrup until mixture evenly moistens and it holds together when squeezed between your fingers. Turn out onto confectioners' sugar–dusted countertop and knead until smooth. Wrap in plastic wrap and let sit overnight to allow almond oils to distribute evenly and make marzipan easier to work with.

3. Wipe the mold with a clean soft dishcloth to remove any dust. Sprinkle insides of mold with confectioners' sugar. Start pressing marzipan firmly into one of the mold halves with your fingers. Turn mold over to ensure marzipan is filling out pig shape. Keep adding and pressing marzipan into mold.

4. To make a flat-backed pig, press marzipan until it is just above the back of the mold. Use the edge of a bench scraper or icing spatula to trim marzipan until level with back of mold. The pig is then ready to unmold.

5. To unmold, gently flex the mold to pop out the pig. If that doesn't work, insert the tip of a sharp knife along the bottom of the mold. Gently pry the pig out of the mold.

6. To make a 3-D pig, simply repeat Steps 3 and 4 with second half of mold, but allow marzipan to be slightly raised above the open edge of the mold. Press both mold halves together very firmly.

7. Cradle one half of the plastic mold in your palm and lift other half off. If it does not immediately release, wiggle it and/or tap the outside of the mold gently with the handle of a bench scraper or icing spatula. Once it is off, gently palm marzipan pig, flip over, and release second half. Trim any seams with a paring knife, if necessary. Repeat molding procedure of choice until marzipan is used up.

8. If you wish to color the pigs, simply brush powder food coloring onto them, using a clean brush for each color and taking care to keep the colored areas separate so that the colors do not bleed.

Candy Tidbits

The pig halves are as cute as the whole pig. Either way, you can present them in little baskets filled with green-tinted "grass" (coconut). See the Candy Tidbits on page 77 for coconut instructions.

Chestnuts in Yam Paste
(Kuri Kinton)

▷●◁ **HOLIDAY** *Japanese New Year*

▷●◁ **TYPE** *Spoon sweet*　　▷●◁ **HABITAT** *Japan*

▷●◁ **DESCRIPTION** *Pretty yellow chestnuts are presented in a rice wine–sweetened sweet potato puree to honor the Japanese New Year, a three-day celebration.*

▷●◁ **FIELD NOTES** *There is no getting around the fact that for American and most European palates the desserts and sweets of Japan are unusual. They are not very sweet, are often based on vegetables and beans, and have interesting forms, such as the sweet here, which you eat with a spoon—the only one in this book! If you can find a* satsuma imo, *which is a red-skinned, golden-fleshed "yam," then by all means use it, as it is traditional. Many thanks to my Japan-based new friend, Elizabeth Andoh, who first published a version of this recipe in* At Home with Japanese Cooking *(Knopf, 1980). Elizabeth says that although these are a traditional Japanese New Year's treat, they might be more appreciated by Western palates served along a holiday turkey as a side dish!*

▷●◁ **LIFESPAN** *1 month refrigerated in airtight container*

Yield: *about 12 servings*

✿ INGREDIENTS

One 13-ounce can or bottle yellow
    chestnuts in syrup (see Candy Tidbits)
1¼ pounds sweet potatoes, peeled and
    cut into ½-inch cubes

½ cup granulated sugar
2 tablespoons mirin (sweetened rice wine)

✿ DIRECTIONS

1. Drain chestnuts, reserving ¼ cup of the
syrup. Cut any large chestnuts in half;
they should be comfortably bite-size,
but still round.

2. Place sweet potatoes in a large
saucepan and cover with cold water.
Cover pot and bring to a boil over
medium-high heat. Turn heat down to
medium and partially uncover. Simmer
until they are fork-tender, about 12
minutes.

3. Drain sweet potatoes and place in a
food processor fitted with a metal
blade. Process until smooth. Scrape
mixture into a strainer set over
a bowl and force mixture
through. Discard any fibrous
pieces left in strainer. You
should end up with about 2
cups silky smooth puree.

4. Place puree in a medium-size saucepan;
stir in sugar and reserved syrup. Bring
to a simmer over medium heat, whisking occasionally, cooking until sugar
dissolves, about 5 minutes. Remove
from heat and stir in mirin and chestnuts. Allow to cool to room temperature, stirring occasionally to release
heat. Present a couple of chestnuts with
some puree in a small, attractive dish,
offered with a spoon. Sweet may be
served at room temperature or chilled.

Candy Tidbits

The chestnuts and mirin can
be found in well-stocked Asian
food stores and large supermarkets.
Sometimes the chestnuts come in
smaller cans; you just need to end
up with 1¼ cups of chestnuts.
The label might say *kuri no
kanro ni.*

Giant Chocolate Kiss

🍬 **HOLIDAY** *Valentine's Day*

🍬 **TYPE** *Molded candy*   🍬 **HABITAT** *United States*

🍬 **DESCRIPTION** *This is a huge version of the little chocolate kisses we all grew up with. It is solid milk chocolate wrapped in foil, with a special message written on a strip that is mostly encased inside the wrapping, but peeks out of the top and helps the lucky recipient remove the foil.*

🍬 **FIELD NOTES** *The famous little Hershey's Kiss has been made since 1907, and more than 30 million of them are produced every day. Here I suggest you make one large treat for a special someone. My recipe is molded in a funnel, so it will not be perfectly shaped like a store-bought version, but it will definitely be close enough for the receiver to get the gist.*

🍬 **LIFESPAN** *1 month refrigerated*

Yield: *1 humongous kiss*

Tools: *One 2-cup Pyrex measuring cup • 2 cups dry rice, beans, or popcorn kernels •
One 10-ounce metal or plastic funnel (about 4³/₄ inches wide across opening and .
5³/₄ inches high) • Plastic wrap and rubber band • One ¹/₃ x 9-inch strip of paper •
One 12 x 18-inch piece aluminum foil*

⊱●⊰ INGREDIENTS

18 ounces couverture milk chocolate (see page 10), finely chopped

⊱●⊰ DIRECTIONS

1. Fill the measuring cup with dry rice; set aside.

2. Wrap a small piece of plastic wrap around the bottom of the funnel's opening and secure it with the rubber band. Nestle the funnel down into rice in measuring cup (the rice will hold it steady) and make sure it is level.

3. Temper chocolate according to the directions on page 14 and slowly pour into funnel almost all the way to the top (leaving about ¹/₈ inch at the top).

4. Let chocolate set until it reaches room temperature, then refrigerate until completely firm, about 4 hours, or overnight.

5. Meanwhile, write a personal note on the first 4 inches of the strip of paper, which will be hidden by the foil. On the other end of the paper, write something like "Open me!", "Look inside!", "For you," or whatever you like.

6. Once chocolate is set, unmold "kiss" by rapping the open end of the funnel somewhat firmly on the counter. The "kiss" should pop out. If not, just repeat rapping on the table.

7. Place foil on counter and place "kiss" in center. Place strip of paper alongside "kiss" with private message near bottom. Bring up edges of foil and wrap it up and around the chocolate, forming it into shape with your hands. The top can be twisted and angled slightly to the side; the top of the message will be peeking out.

Chocolate-Covered Cherries

>●< **HOLIDAY** *Valentine's Day*

>●< **TYPE** *Hand-formed candy*   >●< **HABITAT** *United States*

>●< **DESCRIPTION** *These are the most elegant—and time-consuming—candies in the book. They are a labor of love! They feature Morello cherries that have been soaked in kirsch and then wrapped in a cherry-flavored fondant and double dipped in bittersweet chocolate. Many chocolate-covered cherry recipes use maraschino cherries, but I have chosen a less sweet cherry.*

>●< **FIELD NOTES** *This recipe is a project. There are many steps that must be followed precisely, or else your cherries will leak through the chocolate (the most common problem) or have an odd shape if you don't take care when double dipping. But if you follow through, you will be rewarded with absolutely scrumptious, elegant candies. Note that the cherries must dry overnight in the middle of the recipe and that the candies must "ripen" in the refrigerator for at least a week for the fondant to liquefy within the chocolate shell.*

>●< **LIFESPAN** *1 month refrigerated in airtight container in single layers separated by waxed or parchment paper*

Yield: *about 70 cherries, depending on size*

❧●❧ INGREDIENTS

One 1-pound 9-ounce jar Morello
cherries in syrup (about 2 cups of
cherries without syrup)
$^1/_4$ cup kirsch
$^1/_4$ cup ($^1/_2$ stick) unsalted butter, at room
temperature, cut into pieces
1 tablespoon light corn syrup
$2^1/_4$ cups to $2^3/_4$ cups confectioners' sugar,
sifted

3 pounds
couverture
bittersweet chocolate (see page 10),
finely chopped
70 small fluted paper cups (red, silver, or
gold look great)

Candy Tidbits

If you would like to make these
as professional as possible, order an
additive called Invertase from Sweet
Celebrations (see Resources). Add
$^1/_8$ teaspoon to the fondant while you
are beating it. It will help it liquefy
better during the 1-week
storage stage.

❧●❧ DIRECTIONS

1. Place a cooling rack over a jelly-roll
   pan. Drain cherries, reserving syrup,
   and place in a medium-size saucepan.
   Add $^1/_4$ cup cherry syrup and the
   kirsch. Bring to a boil over medium
   heat; remove from heat and allow to
   cool to room temperature. Remove
   cherries from syrup, reserving syrup,
   and spread cherries on rack so they are
   not touching. Allow to dry at room
   temperature overnight.

2. In a large bowl with an electric mixer
   on medium-high speed, beat butter,
   corn syrup, and 1 tablespoon cherry
   soaking liquid until smooth and
   creamy, about 2 minutes. Beat in about
   2 cups confectioners' sugar on low
   speed until thick and creamy, scraping
   down bowl once or twice. Keep adding
   sugar and beating until mixture is no
   longer sticky and just stiff enough to be
   handled.

3. Line a jelly-roll pan with aluminum
   foil. Roll $^1/_2$-teaspoon portions of sugar
   mixture (fondant) into balls; flatten
   each with your fingers into a thin
   round and wrap that around a cherry,
   completely encircling it, and place on
   prepared pan. Repeat with remaining
   cherries, dipping fingers and hands in

   confectioners' sugar to keep fondant
   from sticking. Refrigerate fondant-
   covered cherries for 30 minutes.

4. Meanwhile, temper chocolate according to the directions on page 14. Line a
   jelly-roll pan with aluminum foil, shiny
   side up, smoothing out any wrinkles,
   or line the pan with a piece of acetate.
   Dip cherries one at a time in the melted
   chocolate until completely coated,
   using your fingers, 2 forks, or chocolate dipping tools. Allow excess chocolate to drip back into the pot, taking
   extra care to make this initial dipping
   as thin and even as possible. Place cherries on the prepared pan.

5. Refrigerate until firm, about 20 minutes. If the cherries have developed a
   "foot," chocolate that might have
   dripped down around the cherry and
   pooled on the pan, trim it carefully
   with a sharp knife before re-dipping.
   One by one, dip the cherries in the
   chocolate again, taking care to keep the
   shape as round as possible. Refrigerate
   until completely firm.

6. Place in fluted paper cups in an airtight
   container and refrigerate for at least 1
   week before serving.

Chocolate Hazelnut Italian Kisses

⋙●⋘ **HOLIDAY** *Valentine's Day*

⋙●⋘ **TYPE** *Hand-formed candy*   ⋙●⋘ **HABITAT** *Italy and United States*

⋙●⋘ **DESCRIPTION** *Do you like the Italian chocolate candy known as Baci? They are a chocolate and hazelnut truffle-like confection whose name translates to "kisses." These candies are a homemade version and will satisfy chocolate and hazelnut lovers everywhere. The commercial Baci are individually wrapped in foil, so that is how these are presented as well.*

⋙●⋘ **FIELD NOTES** *As with any chocolate-based candy (with some exceptions in the kiddie realm), the quality of the chocolate is paramount. For this candy I prefer the richly flavored milk chocolate known as Grand Lait by Michel Cluizel.*

⋙●⋘ **LIFESPAN** *1 month refrigerated in airtight container*

Yield: *50 kisses*

⊱●⊰ INGREDIENTS

6 ounces couverture milk chocolate (see page 10), finely chopped

1 pound plus 4 ounces couverture bittersweet chocolate (see page 10), finely chopped

1 cup heavy cream

3 tablespoons unsalted butter, cut into small pieces

1 cup toasted skinned hazelnuts (see page 16), finely ground

Unsweetened Dutch-processed cocoa powder

50 whole toasted skinned hazelnuts (see page 16)

50 small square foil candy wrappers

⊱●⊰ DIRECTIONS

1. Place milk chocolate and 4 ounces bittersweet chocolate in a large heat-proof bowl.

2. Heat cream in saucepan over medium heat until it just comes to a boil. Pour over chocolates and allow to sit for 5 minutes; the hot cream should melt the chocolate. Stir until smooth, then stir in butter until combined. Stir in ground nuts. Allow to cool to room temperature, whisking occasionally to incorporate a bit of air and lighten mixture. Refrigerate until firm enough to roll, about 3 hours.

3. Coat your hands with cocoa powder and roll mixture into 1-inch balls. Press 1 whole nut into each ball, leaving it poking out of the top; they should not be buried inside.

4. Temper remaining bittersweet chocolate according to the directions on page 14. Line a jelly-roll pan with aluminum foil, shiny side up, smoothing out any wrinkles, or line the pan with a piece of acetate. Dip "kisses" one at a time into the melted chocolate until completely coated, using your fingers, 2 forks, or chocolate dipping tools. Allow excess chocolate to drip back into the pot. Place "kisses" carefully on the lined pan, nut side up. Refrigerate until firm. Wrap in foil wrappers. Enjoy at room temperature.

Bittersweet Chocolate Truffles

>●< **HOLIDAY** *Valentine's Day, Christmas*

>●< **TYPE** *Hand-formed candy*   >●< **HABITAT** *United States and Europe*

>●< **DESCRIPTION** *When I think of eating chocolate, I think of truffles. With just a little heavy cream to enhance the texture, there is nothing else standing in the way of pure chocolate bliss. It should go without saying that you should use the very best chocolate you can find and afford. The informal outer coating of cocoa powder makes these particularly easy to make. The Dutch-processed is darker; the natural is lighter. I think it looks pretty and natural to have variation, so I use both.*

>●< **FIELD NOTES** *Dark chocolate truffles are the ne plus ultra of truffles, and they are popular in many countries during various parts of the year. In America, truffles are often given on Valentine's Day. In Europe, particularly in France and Italy, you will find them in fine candy shops year-round, but they are especially popular at Christmastime. By the way, they are supposed to mimic the savory truffles that grow beneath trees—that's why you don't have to make perfect little balls. Rather, they should have an organic, rustic look to them.*

>●< **LIFESPAN** *2 weeks refrigerated in airtight container in single layers separated by waxed or parchment paper*

Yield: *80 truffles*

✑●◀ INGREDIENTS

1²/₃ cups heavy cream
1 pound bittersweet couverture chocolate
(see page 10), very finely chopped

Unsweetened Dutch-processed cocoa
powder
Natural cocoa powder
80 small fluted paper cups (optional)

✑●◀ DIRECTIONS

1. Heat cream in a large saucepan over medium heat until it just comes to a simmer. Remove from heat and immediately sprinkle chocolate into cream. Allow to sit for 5 minutes; the hot cream should melt the chocolate. Stir very gently, so as not to incorporate air, until smooth. If chocolate isn't melting, place the saucepan over very low heat and stir until smooth, but take care not to let it get too hot or burn.

2. Pour mixture, now called a ganache, into a shallow bowl and allow to cool at room temperature until firm enough to roll, preferably overnight.

3. Coat your hands with cocoa powder (either kind) and roll ganache into ³/₄-inch balls. They should be roundish, but do not need to be perfect.

4. Place each kind of cocoa powder in a separate small bowl. Toss truffles in one of the cocoas. Place in fluted paper cups, if desired. Enjoy at room temperature.

Candy Tidbits

The overnight rest for the ganache not only allows it to firm up, but it also allows flavors to develop and yields the most silken texture. If you would like to hasten the cooling process for any truffle recipe, refrigerate the ganache just until firm enough to roll, most likely about 4 hours.

Liqueur-Enhanced Chocolate Truffles

🍬 **HOLIDAY** *Valentine's Day, Christmas*

🍬 **TYPE** *Hand-molded candy*   🍬 **HABITAT** *United States and Europe*

🍬 **DESCRIPTION** *These bittersweet chocolate truffles can be made with any compatible liqueur. I suggest Grand Marnier, Kahlúa, or Chambord for starters.*

🍬 **FIELD NOTES** *These truffles are very similar to the Bittersweet Chocolate Truffles on page 36, except that they have a little less cream in the filling to allow for the liquid provided from the liqueur, which softens the ganache somewhat—and they are also dipped in a chocolate shell.*

🍬 **LIFESPAN** *2 weeks refrigerated in airtight container in single layers separated by waxed or parchment paper*

Yield: *about 90 truffles*

⋙●⋘ INGREDIENTS

1½ cups heavy cream
2 pounds plus 4 ounces couverture
bittersweet chocolate (see page 10),
very finely chopped

4 to 6 tablespoons liqueur, such as
Grand Marnier, Kahlúa, or Chambord
Unsweetened Dutch-processed cocoa
powder
90 small fluted paper cups (optional)

⋙●⋘ DIRECTIONS

1. Heat cream in a large saucepan over medium heat until it just comes to a simmer.

2. Remove from heat and immediately sprinkle 1 pound chocolate into cream. Allow to sit for 5 minutes; the hot cream should melt the chocolate. Stir very gently, so as not to incorporate air, until smooth. If chocolate isn't melting, place saucepan over very low heat and stir until smooth, but take care not to let it get too hot or burn. Stir in liqueur, to taste, until incorporated.

3. Pour mixture, now called a ganache, into a shallow bowl and allow to cool at room temperature, then refrigerate until firm enough to roll, preferably overnight.

4. Coat your hands with cocoa powder and roll ganache into ¾-inch balls. These should be as round as possible but do not need to be perfect. Place in a single layer on a jelly-roll pan and chill until very firm. (Type of chocolate, ambient temperature, and other variables will determine the length of chilling time, typically anywhere from 30 minutes to 2 hours. Overnight refrigeration will also work.)

5. Temper remaining chocolate according to the directions on page 14. Line a jelly-roll pan with aluminum foil, shiny side up, smoothing out any wrinkles, or line the pan with a piece of acetate. Dip truffles one at a time in the melted chocolate, tossing back and forth with your fingers, 2 forks, or chocolate dipping tools. Allow excess chocolate to drip back into the pot. Place truffles carefully on the lined pan. Refrigerate until firm. Place in fluted paper cups, if desired, and enjoy at room temperature.

Candy Tidbits

You can embellish these further— add a cube of candied orange peel to the tops of truffles flavored with Grand Marnier. Sprinkle Kahlúa-flavored truffles with instant espresso powder. If flavored with Chambord, they look nice with a sprinkling of red or pink colored sugar. The toppings should be ready to go while the dipped truffles are wet, and applied to the moist truffles. Any leftover tempered chocolate can be allowed to harden and reused.

Milk Chocolate Truffles

HOLIDAY *Valentine's Day, Christmas*

TYPE *Hand-formed candy*   **HABITAT** *United States*

DESCRIPTION *These truffles feature milk chocolate and cream rolled into a ball and enrobed in milk chocolate. That's just a fancy way of saying they are dipped in melted chocolate until it completely coats the truffle.*

FIELD NOTES *Milk chocolate is very popular, and these days there are more kinds than ever to choose from. There are even milk chocolates out there that are referred to as "extreme" milk chocolate, which is simply milk chocolate with a high percentage of cocoa mass—a darker-style milk chocolate! I like Michel Cluizel's Grand Lait, which has 45 percent cocoa mass.*

RELATED SPECIES *For Mocha Truffles, dissolve 2 tablespoons instant espresso powder in the hot cream before adding the chocolate.*

LIFESPAN *2 weeks refrigerated in airtight container in single layers separated by waxed or parchment paper*

Yield: *75 truffles*

❧●❧ INGREDIENTS

1⅓ cups heavy cream
2 pounds couverture milk chocolate (see page 10), very finely chopped, divided

Unsweetened Dutch-processed cocoa powder
75 small fluted paper cups (optional)

❧●❧ DIRECTIONS

1. Heat cream in a large saucepan over medium heat until it just comes to a simmer. Remove from heat and immediately sprinkle 1 pound chocolate into cream. Allow to sit for 5 minutes; the hot cream should melt the chocolate. Stir very gently, so as not to incorporate air, until smooth. If chocolate isn't melting, place the saucepan over very low heat and stir until smooth, but take care not to let it get too hot or burn.

2. Pour mixture, now called a ganache, into a shallow bowl and allow to cool at room temperature until firm enough to roll, preferably overnight.

3. Coat your hands with cocoa powder and roll ganache into ¾-inch balls. These should be as round as possible but do not need to be perfect. Place in a single layer on a jelly-roll pan and chill until very firm. (Type of chocolate, ambient temperature, and other variables will determine the length of chilling time, typically anywhere from 30 minutes to 2 hours. Overnight refrigeration will also work.)

4. Temper remaining milk chocolate according to the directions on page 14. Line a jelly-roll pan with aluminum foil, shiny side up, smoothing out any wrinkles, or line the pan with a piece of acetate. Dip truffles one at a time in melted milk chocolate, tossing back and forth with your fingers, 2 forks, or chocolate dipping tools. Allow excess chocolate to drip back into the pot. Place truffles carefully on the lined pan. Refrigerate until firm. Place in fluted paper cups, if desired. Enjoy at room temperature.

> **Candy Tidbits**
>
> If too much chocolate is left on the truffle after dipping, it will pool around the base of the candy, making what is called a "foot." It is unsightly and thick and best avoided, so take time during dipping to get the thinnest possible coating on the truffles. If you end up getting a "foot" anyway, you can try trimming it with a sharp knife after the truffle has firmed up.

Gilded White Chocolate Truffles

 HOLIDAY *Valentine's Day, Christmas*

....

 TYPE *Hand-formed candy*   **HABITAT** *United States*

....

 DESCRIPTION *These truffles are made of white chocolate and cream and are for all those white chocolate fanatics. The crowning touch of gold is optional, but very special! The gold will cost you about $30 a package, but you will only use a tiny portion and the remainder will keep indefinitely. Just make sure to store it in an airtight container.*

....

 FIELD NOTES *According to the Food and Drug Administration, chocolate must contain chocolate liquor, which is derived from mashed cocoa beans, so white chocolate, which has no chocolate liquor, technically is not chocolate at all! To find a high-quality white chocolate, look for cocoa butter as the listed fat, which will give it a chocolatey flavor and aroma.*

....

 RELATED SPECIES *There are many flavor variations to try: Add ¹/₂ teaspoon orange, lemon, lime, tangerine, or grapefruit oil to the ganache. Make Cappuccino Truffles by adding 2 tablespoons instant espresso powder and ¹/₄ teaspoon ground cinnamon to the ganache. Dust the tops lightly with a mixture of cinnamon and cocoa.*

....

 LIFESPAN *2 weeks refrigerated in airtight container in single layers separated by waxed or parchment paper*

Yield: *90 truffles*

Tools: *Tweezers*

⊳●⊰ INGREDIENTS

³/₄ cup plus 3 tablespoons heavy cream

2 pounds plus 2 ounces couverture white chocolate (see page 10), very finely chopped

Confectioners' sugar

22-karat gold leaf (see Resources)

90 small fluted paper cups (optional)

⊳●⊰ DIRECTIONS

1. Heat cream in a large saucepan over medium heat until it just comes to a simmer. Remove from heat and immediately sprinkle 1 pound chocolate into cream. Allow to sit for 5 minutes; the hot cream should melt the chocolate. Stir very gently, so as not to incorporate air, until smooth. If chocolate isn't melting, place the saucepan over very low heat and stir until smooth, but take care not to let it get too hot or burn.

2. Pour mixture, now called a ganache, into a shallow bowl and allow to cool at room temperature, then refrigerate until firm enough to roll, preferably overnight.

3. Coat your hands with confectioners' sugar and roll ganache into ³/₄-inch balls. These should be as round as possible but do not need to be perfect. Place in a single layer on a jelly-roll pan and chill until very firm. (Type of

chocolate, ambient temperature, and other variables will determine the length of chilling time, typically anywhere from 30 minutes to 2 hours. Overnight refrigeration will also work.)

4. Meanwhile, temper remaining white chocolate according to the directions on page 14. Line a jelly-roll pan with aluminum foil, shiny side up, smoothing out any wrinkles, or line the pan with a piece of acetate. Dip truffles one at a time into the melted white chocolate, tossing back and forth with your fingers, 2 forks, or chocolate dipping tools. Allow excess chocolate to drip back into the pot. Place truffles carefully on the lined pan. Use tweezers to pick up little bits of gold leaf and place on wet chocolate (it will adhere). Refrigerate until firm. Place in fluted paper cups, if desired. Enjoy at room temperature.

Cinnamon Fireball Candies

῾●ῼ **HOLIDAY** *Valentine's Day*

῾●ῼ **TYPE** *Molded or poured candy*   ῾●ῼ **HABITAT** *United States*

῾●ῼ **DESCRIPTION** *These spicy hot treats are made with cinnamon oil and taste kind of like fireball candies.*

῾●ῼ **FIELD NOTES** *Warning: Cinnamon oil is very potent. There is a fine line between these being enjoyably hot and so hot that they can feel like they are burning your lips. I have erred on the side of caution and used a small quantity of oil. Increase as desired—and at your own risk! I use LorAnn cinnamon oil. I make these in 3-D round molds from Sweet Celebrations or Kitchen Krafts, but in order to do that, you need a lot of molds. You could also just pour all the candy out onto a jelly-roll pan lined with well-oiled aluminum foil. My suggestion is to buy one set of molds, use them, and then pour the remainder on the foil to break into pieces.*

῾●ῼ **LIFESPAN** *1 week at room temperature in airtight container, broken pieces in single layers separated by waxed or parchment paper*

Yield: *about 6 "fireballs" and about 20 pieces of candy*

Tools: *4-cup measuring cup with spout • Small funnel • One 1-inch Hard Candy Ball Sucker Mold*

INGREDIENTS

1³/₄ cups granulated sugar
¹/₂ cup corn syrup
¹/₂ cup water
1¹/₂ teaspoons cinnamon oil

1 teaspoon red liquid food coloring
6 small square candy wrappers or cellophane

DIRECTIONS

1. Wipe the mold with a clean soft dishcloth to remove any dust. Assemble mold according to manufacturer's instructions. Line a jelly-roll pan with aluminum foil, smoothing out any wrinkles. Coat foil with nonstick cooking spray.

2. Stir together sugar, corn syrup, and water in a medium-size deep saucepan. Cook over medium heat to 300°F (hard-crack stage) and immediately remove from heat.

3. Allow bubbling to subside, then add cinnamon oil and coloring. The cinnamon fumes can be potent, so don't lean over the pot. Swirl pot to incorporate and until color is distributed evenly. Transfer mixture to a measuring cup with a spout.

4. Use a small funnel to slowly pour mixture into molds all the way to the top. Pour remainder onto prepared pan. Allow to cool completely. The exterior of the molds should be completely cool before unmolding, about 30 minutes. Unmold and wrap in cellophane wrappers. The candy poured out on the pan can be broken into pieces.

Champagne and Cherry Heart Lollipops

♥ **HOLIDAY** *Valentine's Day*

♥ **TYPE** *Molded candy*   ♥ **HABITAT** *United States*

♥ **DESCRIPTION** *This is a sophisticated lollipop. Not only is there a lolli within a lolli, but the flavors, cherry and champagne, are grown up. That said, there is nothing alcoholic in these, so they may be enjoyed by children as well.*

♥ **FIELD NOTES** *You need some special equipment and ingredients to make these. First, order the molds and heart quins (the little heart-shaped candies sprinkled in the center) from Sweet Celebrations (see Resources). The molds are called Combo Heart LolliMolds Sucker Molds (they even come with sticks). The mold set comes with 4 large hearts and 6 small. This is why you will end up with 4 large heart-within-a-heart suckers and 2 extra-small hearts, and also why you might have some extra lollipop mixture. You also need two flavorings, champagne and cherry, which can be ordered from Sweet Celebrations as well, or directly from LorAnn Oils (see Resources).*

♥ **LIFESPAN** *1 month at room temperature*

Yield: *4 heart-within-a-heart lollipops and 2 extra-small hearts*

Tools: *1 set Combo Heart LolliMolds Sucker Molds ● 6 clear candy bags ● 6 decorative twist ties or pieces of ribbon*

⮞●⮜ INGREDIENTS

Small hearts:
½ cup granulated sugar
2 tablespoons light corn syrup
2 tablespoons water
Generous ¼ teaspoon cherry flavoring
Red heart quins

Large hearts:
1½ cups granulated sugar
6 tablespoons light corn syrup
6 tablespoons water
1 teaspoon champagne flavoring

⮞●⮜ DIRECTIONS

1. Wipe the molds with a clean soft dish-cloth to remove any dust. Coat a flat jelly-roll pan and the insides of the molds with nonstick cooking spray.

2. Assemble small heart molds according to manufacturer's instructions. Squeeze the molds shut against and around the sticks; slide the clips into place to secure molds. Adjust sticks so that about ½ inch is just inside the heart-shaped part of the molds. (The molds come with visual directions, and all of this will make sense when you see them.) Place on jelly-roll pan.

3. To make small hearts, stir together sugar, corn syrup, and water in a medium-size saucepan. Bring to a boil over medium-high heat, swirling the pan once or twice. Cook to 300°F (hard-crack stage) and immediately remove from heat. Allow bubbling to subside, then add cherry flavoring and swirl to incorporate. Use a teaspoon to place mixture in molds, coming about one-third of the way up the sides of the molds. Sprinkle a few red heart quins into the mold, then add more sugar mixture to come up about two-thirds of the way to the top of the molds.

4. Allow lollipops to harden, about 15 minutes. Slide down clips and release and remove molds.

5. Assemble larger molds with small heart lollipop on its stick inside each large heart mold. Make sure clip is in place and that small heart lollipop is nestled down against the bottom of the inside of large heart mold.

6. Combine ingredients for large hearts together as described above and bring to 300°F (hard-crack stage); immediately remove from heat. Allow bubbling to subside, then swirl in champagne flavoring. Allow mixture to cool slightly, but it must remain fluid. Spoon mixture into the large molds, up to the top edge. The small heart should become enveloped.

7. Allow lollipops to harden, about 25 minutes. Slide down clips and release and remove molds. Cool completely, then place in bags and seal with a twist tie.

Candy Tidbits

It is vitally important that you have a perfectly flat pan, or the open-backed lollipop molds will leak.

Golden Heart Passion Pops

⊁●≼ **HOLIDAY** *Valentine's Day, weddings*

⊁●≼ **TYPE** *Molded candy*   ⊁●≼ **HABITAT** *United States*

⊁●≼ **DESCRIPTION** *Here is another sophisticated, all-grown-up lollipop. A voluptuous, rounded heart shape features passion-fruit flavor and flecks of real gold leaf. They are a very adult treat, but every child I offered these to loved them as well.*

⊁●≼ **FIELD NOTES** *I love, love, love these lollies. They are sweet and tart (kind of like love) and very fancy looking with the gold leaf, which is edible as long as it is at least 22 karats. Look for it in art-supply stores or mail order it from Beryl's (see Resources). These are great for Valentine's Day, but equally welcomed as a bridal shower or wedding party favor. I used LorAnn molds, and the passion-fruit flavoring can be ordered from www.getsuckered.com. The Wilton Petal Pink paste (see Resources) is the perfect soft color.*

⊁●≼ **LIFESPAN** *1 month at room temperature*

Yield: *10 passion pops*

Tools: *2 LorAnn Heart Sheet Molds ● Ten 4-inch lollipop sticks ● Tweezers ● 10 clear candy bags ● 10 gold twist ties or pieces of ribbon*

⋙●⋘ INGREDIENTS

1½ cups granulated sugar
⅓ cup light corn syrup
⅓ cup water
1½ teaspoons passion-fruit flavoring

Wilton Petal Pink paste food coloring
⅛ teaspoon citric acid
22-karat gold leaf

⋙●⋘ DIRECTIONS

1. Wipe the molds with a clean soft dish-cloth to remove any dust. Lightly coat the insides of the molds with nonstick cooking spray and insert sticks.

2. Stir together sugar, corn syrup, and water in a medium-size saucepan. Bring to a boil over medium-high heat, swirling the pan once or twice. Cook to 300°F (hard-crack stage) and immediately remove from heat. Allow bubbling to subside; check temperature and proceed when it lowers to 260°F. Add passion-fruit flavoring, half a pea-size ball of paste color, and the citric acid. Swirl pot to incorporate so that the mixture is a very pale pink. Spoon mixture into molds all the way to the top.

3. Allow lollipops to harden, about 25 minutes, then unmold.

4. Pick up bits of gold leaf with tweezers and place pieces here and there on rounded side to decorate (refer to photo). Cool lollipops completely, then place in bags and seal with a twist tie.

Candy Tidbits

Citric acid is a natural fruit acid that adds tang and a pleasant sourness to candies. If you want to turn a sweet hard or creamy candy recipe a little sour, try adding ⅛ teaspoon to every 2 cups of sugar. Always add it to a mixture that has cooled to 260°F (or one that will not be heated above this temperature), as otherwise the tartness will diminish.

Marzipan-Stuffed Fruit and Nuts

✻●✻ **HOLIDAY** *Purim, weddings*

✻●✻ **TYPE** *Hand-formed candy*   ✻●✻ **HABITAT** *Israel and North Africa*

✻●✻ **DESCRIPTION** *Marzipan that has been flavored with orange zest and orange-flavored liqueur or orange juice is both sandwiched between nut halves and stuffed into dates.*

✻●✻ **FIELD NOTES** *Marzipan, which is simply a sweetened almond paste, is found in many cultures, and confections similar to these are made in many areas of the world and served at various times. These are often served at Purim and at weddings or showers and are referred to as "bread of Mordecai." Use the orange juice to make these more kid friendly.*

✻●✻ **LIFESPAN** *1 month refrigerated in airtight container in single layers separated by waxed or parchment paper*

Yield: *24 filled dates and nuts*

✦●✦ INGREDIENTS

12 plump dates, such as Medjool
8 ounces almond paste
3 tablespoons confectioners' sugar
1 teaspoon orange zest

1 ½ teaspoons Grand Marnier or orange juice
24 toasted walnut halves (see page 16; make sure the nut halves are "whole")

✦●✦ DIRECTIONS

1. Make a lengthwise slit in each date, making sure not to cut through the back/bottom of the date. Remove and discard pits, if there are any.

2. Place almond paste, confectioners' sugar, orange zest, and liquid of choice in a small bowl and stir together with a wooden spoon or your fingers. I find it best to mix together with my fingers. Just get in there and work it!

3. Use your fingers to pick up a bit of the mixture and roll it into a small log shape. Press a marzipan log into each date, allowing some filling to still show (see photo). For the walnuts, roll a small ball of marzipan mixture and sandwich it between two nut halves, pressing the nuts together to slightly flatten the marzipan.

Candy Tidbits

Other fruits and nuts lend themselves to this recipe: Try pecans and apricots, figs, or prunes.

Poppy Seed Candy (Monlach)

 **HOLIDAY** *Purim*

....

 **TYPE** *Poured candy*    **HABITAT** *Israel and United States*

....

 **DESCRIPTION** *The unique, faintly nutty flavor of poppy seeds shines through in these sticky candies, as does the flavor of honey.*

....

 **FIELD NOTES** *There are various poppy seed candies popular at Purim, some with the seeds first soaked in water and others featuring ground seeds. Some add raisins and nuts or spices. What they have in common is their origin. A Jewish noblewoman, Esther, was slated to marry a non-Jew. While residing in his palace, she nibbled on poppy seeds so as not to partake of any nonkosher foods. These candies are often cut into diamond shapes, but I find them sticky to work with and prefer to roll them into little log shapes. Also, you could use an oiled jelly-roll pan, but I think the wooden board and water technique works very well with these candies.*

....

 **LIFESPAN** *1 month at room temperature in airtight container*

Yield: *60 candies*

⌘ INGREDIENTS

1 cup poppy seeds
1 cup honey
$^1/_4$ cup granulated sugar
$^1/_2$ teaspoon ground ginger

$^1/_2$ cup whole blanched almonds, finely
ground
60 small square candy wrappers or
cellophane

⌘ DIRECTIONS

1. Rinse a clean, large wooden board with cold water. Allow water droplets to remain on board.

2. Place half the poppyseeds in a food grinder or clean coffee grinder and process until finely ground. Place honey and sugar together in a medium-size saucepan and stir to combine. Bring to a boil over medium-high heat; stir in all the poppyseeds (ground and whole), ginger, and nuts. Continue boiling and bring to 260°F (hard-ball stage).

3. Immediately scrape out onto prepared board and spread into a rectangle (about 12 x 8 inches) about $^1/_3$-inch thick; the thickness is what is most important. Let mixture sit at room temperature until cooled off a bit; score pieces with a knife while still warm to a size of about $^3/_4$ x $1^1/_2$ inches. Cool completely, about 2 hours.

4. Use a bench scraper to cut straight down into the candy, dividing it into pieces. The candy might be very sticky and the pieces will not necessarily keep their exact shape. Gently shape them into logs, or use the bench scraper to cut the candy into diamond-shaped pieces, then wrap them individually in wrappers or cellophane.

Sweet Wine Chocolate Apricot Balls

>●< **HOLIDAY** *Purim*

>●< **TYPE** *Hand-formed candy*   >●< **HABITAT** *Israel and United States*

>●< **DESCRIPTION** *These candies are very easy to make but have a very sophisticated flavor due to the addition of sweet wine. Sweet wine is a customary addition to the Purim table and is what connects these candies with the holiday. They are a simple combination of cookie crumbs, wine-soaked apricots, cocoa, and chocolate enriched with butter and rolled in toasted almonds.*

>●< **FIELD NOTES** *When it comes to Jewish foods and customs, I always turn to Faye Levy. She is not only a prolific cookbook writer, but is also incredibly generous with her knowledge. These candies are based on ones made by Faye and her family; a version of them is featured in her cookbook* 1,000 Jewish Recipes *(Wiley, 2000). She mentions that using raisins instead of apricots would also be traditional. She likes vanilla cookie crumbs; her mom uses chocolate. I chose to use a shortbread for its buttery-ness. By the way, the idea of using Sauternes is mine; Faye wanted me to make sure to mention that a kosher wine would be most appropriate.*

>●< **LIFESPAN** *1½ months refrigerated in airtight container in single layers separated by waxed or parchment paper*

Yield: *about 42 balls*

INGREDIENTS

1/2 cup dried apricots

1/2 cup sweet wine, such as Sauternes

4 ounces semisweet chocolate, finely chopped

1 tablespoon sugar

1 tablespoon unsweetened Dutch-processed cocoa powder

4 tablespoons (1/2 stick) unsalted butter, cut into pieces

1 cup cookie crumbs made from about 20 Lorna Doone cookies

1 1/4 cups toasted sliced natural almonds (see page 16), roughly chopped

42 small fluted paper cups (optional)

DIRECTIONS

1. In a food processor fitted with a metal blade, finely mince the apricots. Stir together apricots, wine, chocolate, sugar, and cocoa powder in a medium-size heavy saucepan. Cook over medium heat, stirring frequently, until chocolate melts and sugar dissolves, about 5 minutes.

2. Remove from heat and add butter 1 piece at a time, stirring until melted and absorbed. Stir in cookie crumbs. Scrape mixture into a bowl and chill about 1 hour, or until firm enough to roll.

3. Place nuts in a medium-size bowl. Roll apricot mixture between your palms into 1-inch balls, then roll in nuts. You may place the balls in small fluted paper cups, if desired.

Candy Tidbits

To make this a more kid-friendly treat, use orange juice instead of wine.

Mint Jelly Leaves

🍬 **HOLIDAY** *Vernal equinox*

🍬 **TYPE** *Bar or molded candy*   🍬 **HABITAT** *United States*

🍬 **DESCRIPTION** *Spearmint has a very fresh mint flavor, and here it is showcased in a gorgeous, translucent green leaf-shaped jelly candy. Since these are made with gelatin, they should be refrigerated. The coolness will also accentuate the minty freshness.*

🍬 **FIELD NOTES** *You could make these in rubber molds, in which case the leaves will have an imprint of veins and look very realistic, but you would need many, many molds. My alternative is to mold the candy in a pan and cut out leaf shapes with a small cookie cutter after it is set. You will have some scrap from in between the leaf shapes, which won't be pretty but will taste just as good! If you would rather use molds, see Candy Tidbits for information.*

🍬 **LIFESPAN** *1 week refrigerated in airtight container in single layers separated by waxed or parchment paper*

Yield: *about 36 leaves*

Tools: *1¹/₄-inch leaf-shaped cookie cutter*

⇒●⇐ INGREDIENTS

1³/₄ cups water
2 tablespoons plus 1 teaspoon unflavored
   gelatin
2 cups granulated sugar

¹/₈ to ¹/₄ teaspoon spearmint oil, to your
   taste
Liquid green food coloring
Granulated or superfine sugar for coating

⇒●⇐ DIRECTIONS

1. Generously oil the bottom and sides of a 9-inch square baking pan. Also generously oil a jelly-roll pan; set aside.

2. Stir together ¹/₄ cup water and gelatin in a small bowl. Let sit 5 minutes to soften.

3. Meanwhile, stir together sugar and remaining 1¹/₂ cups water in a medium-size saucepan. Bring to a boil over medium heat, swirling the pot once or twice, cooking until sugar dissolves.

4. Remove from heat and quickly whisk in softened gelatin until it dissolves. Whisk in spearmint oil and 2 drops green coloring.

5. Pour into prepared pan and place on rack to cool to room temperature. Refrigerate until set, about 5 hours.

6. Loosen edges of jelly with sharp tip of a knife; slip a small offset spatula underneath jelly to loosen it. Flip over and unmold onto oiled jelly-roll pan.

7. Lightly oil the cookie cutter. Cut out leaves as close together as possible to reduce scrap. Toss leaves in sugar to coat completely.

Candy Tidbits

If you would like to use molds, I have had success with the small leaf-shaped rubber molds available from Sweet Celebrations (see Resources). Simply pour the mixture into molds, and unmold after the chilling period.

Maple Sugar Leaves

◈ HOLIDAY *Vernal equinox*

◈ TYPE *Bar or molded candy*   **◈ HABITAT** *United States*

◈ DESCRIPTION *If you like pure maple syrup, then you will love these crumbly sweet maple candies. They can be made in any shape, but I thought leaves were most appropriate.*

◈ FIELD NOTES *These are very easy to make and have essentially one ingredient: maple syrup! Make sure to use pure maple syrup, not table syrup, which is artificially flavored. I met someone recently who didn't realize that maple syrup came from trees! I live in New England, so there is no mistaking the real thing. Grade A Light Amber will give you the lightest-colored and -flavored result. Medium and Dark Amber may be used, but the candies will be darker, with a more pronounced flavor.*

◈ LIFESPAN *1 month at room temperature in airtight container in single layers separated by waxed or parchment paper*

Yield: *about 36 leaves (about ¹/₃-inch deep)*
Tools: *1¹/₄-inch maple leaf–shaped cookie cutter*

⋙●⋘ INGREDIENTS

2 cups pure maple syrup
1 teaspoon unsalted butter

⋙●⋘ DIRECTIONS

1. Line an 8-inch square baking pan with aluminum foil so that foil overhangs by a few inches on all sides, smoothing out any wrinkles. Lightly coat foil with nonstick cooking spray.

2. Place maple syrup in a medium-size deep saucepan. Rub butter along inside top edge of the pan; this should help reduce the tendency to boil over.

3. Bring to a simmer over medium heat; watch it carefully as it can boil over easily. Adjust heat as necessary. Cook to 240°F (soft-ball stage). Remove from heat and allow to cool for 5 minutes.

4. Stir gently until mixture turns opaque and begins to develop a grain. It will feel scratchy beneath your spoon, and it will take a few minutes, so be patient. Keep stirring until it lightens and thickens, but do not let it completely set. The mixture should ribbon back on itself when it is ready, and it should feel grainy on your tongue when you taste it.

5. Immediately scrape into prepared pan; allow to set until cool and firm but not completely hard, about 7 minutes. Unmold by pulling foil up and out of pan; peel off foil. Cut out leaf shapes with cookie cutter. There will be scraps, but you can eat those too!

Candy Tidbits

If you would like to form these in individual molds, you can order the ones from Kitchen Krafts (see Resources). There are 20 leaf cavities in 1 plaque. Coat the molds with nonstick cooking spray, spoon mixture into individual cavities, and level off excess by scraping an offset spatula over the top. Allow to harden, then unmold.

Rainbow Chocolate Fish

◗●◖ HOLIDAY *April Fool's Day*   **◗●◖ TYPE** *Molded candy*

◗●◖ HABITAT *France*

◗●◖ DESCRIPTION *These are simply white chocolate fish that have been made in a mold and then painted with dry powder food coloring or edible food color spray.*

◗●◖ FIELD NOTES *You might be wondering what fish and April Fool's Day have to do with one another. In France, April 1 is called* Poisson d'Avril, *or April Fish. As a joke, folks stick a small paper fish on an unsuspecting person's back. The exclamation "poisson d'avril" would be a fitting accompaniment. Here I have translated the custom to food—not to be stuck on anyone's back, but to be eaten and enjoyed. You will need fish-shaped molds. I use versions from both Sweet Celebrations and Tomric, which measure about 1 x 2$\frac{1}{2}$ inches and $^{3}/_{4}$ x 3 inches. The amount of chocolate needed depends on your molds, of course (my fish are about $^{1}/_{4}$ ounce each). You will also need dry powder colors or Wilton's Color Mist in a variety of colors (see Resources). I like green, blue, and orange.*

◗●◖ LIFESPAN *1 month refrigerated in airtight container in single layers separated by waxed or parchment paper*

Yield: *about 26 fish*

Tools: *26 flexible plastic small-fish molds • Small soft artist's paintbrush (if using powder food colorings)*

⇒●⇐ INGREDIENTS

12 ounces couverture white chocolate (see page 10), finely chopped

Dry powder food coloring in blue, green, and orange, or Wilton Color Mist in blue, green, and orange

⇒●⇐ DIRECTIONS

1. Wipe the molds with a clean soft dish-cloth to remove any dust. Temper chocolate according to the directions on page 14. Carefully spoon chocolate into the molds, right up to the top. Use a small offset spatula to scrape off excess. Gently tap the molds on the counter to release any bubbles.

2. Refrigerate until firm, then unmold and place fish, right side up and not touching, on 2 jelly-roll pans.

3. Use a small artist's brush to apply dry powder colors. Try making stripes horizontally, vertically, or diagonally. Two or three colors per fish look best. Be creative!

4. Alternatively, use spray to color fish. Make sure to spray very light layers of color or it will not dry. Allow fish to dry at room temperature for about 20 minutes, or until dry to the touch.

Candy Tidbits

The fish molds come in plaques that hold several fish. They usually come with 10 to 12 fish, but make sure to ask the person you are ordering from how many fish there are per plaque. You could also mention that you are looking for fish molds that use about ¼-ounce of chocolate for each fish. Also, if using the spray food coloring, practice on a piece of white paper to get the feel for how it comes out of the can.

Kitty Crunchies

🍬 **HOLIDAY** *April Fool's Day*

🍬 **TYPE** *Hand-formed candy*   🍬 **HABITAT** *United States*

🍬 **DESCRIPTION** *These are meant to look like kitty poop nestled in kitty litter—and they do! They may look disgusting, but they taste great, as they are a combination of cocoa crisped rice cereal, melted marshmallows, and Grape-Nuts. Kids will love 'em.*

🍬 **FIELD NOTES** *Bring these to a children's party and all the kids will think you are the coolest parent around. The recipe makes enough for two "kitty litter boxes," so that you will have some to take to a party and some to serve at home. I have used 9 x 13-inch baking pans to serve the candy. If you like, you can buy a disposable kitty litter box for even more realism; in that case, the entire recipe can go into the box.*

🍬 **LIFESPAN** *3 days covered with plastic wrap or aluminum foil*

Yield: *2 boxes of "kitty litter" filled with crunchies*

⋙●⋘ INGREDIENTS

20 regular-size marshmallows

1 1/2 tablespoons unsalted butter, cut into 4 pieces

3 cups cocoa-flavored crisped rice cereal

1/3 cup unsweetened Dutch-processed cocoa powder

8 cups Grape-Nuts cereal

1 cup confectioners' sugar

⋙●⋘ DIRECTIONS

1. Place marshmallows and butter in a large microwavable bowl. Heat on high power for 1 minute. Check mixture and microwave further if marshmallows and butter are not melted. Stir together vigorously to combine. Stir in crisped rice cereal until thoroughly combined.

2. Place cocoa powder in a small mixing bowl. Spritz both your palms with nonstick cooking spray. Pick up about 2 tablespoons of candy mixture and compress firmly between your palms. You do want to crush the cereal somewhat. Roll it between your palms into a log shape about 1/2-inch wide. Separate into realistic-looking lengths. Toss in cocoa powder to coat, then pick up again and roll between your palms to remove some of the cocoa powder and give it a more realistic coloring. Repeat with remaining mixture, making various lengths of "poop" to make about 20 pieces.

3. For kitty litter, toss together the Grape-Nuts cereal and confectioners' sugar until thoroughly blended. Divide into two 9 x 13-inch baking pans. Nestle the "poops" in the "kitty litter." They are now ready to offer to unsuspecting friends—or April fools! Cover with plastic wrap or aluminum foil until ready to serve.

Candy Tidbits

You may also melt the marshmallows and butter in a large saucepan on top of the stove over medium heat.

Easter Peepers

🍬 **HOLIDAY** *Easter*

🍬 **TYPE** *Piped candy*   🍬 **HABITAT** *United States*

🍬 **DESCRIPTION** *Here are soft, tender homemade marshmallows, piped into the shapes of chicks to mimic the very popular Peeps Easter candy. I have used yellow food coloring, but of course you may use any color you wish.*

🍬 **FIELD NOTES** *There are two marshmallow recipes in this book. The marshmallow stars, on page 22, contain egg whites; this recipe does not. I have included both so that you have a variety of marshmallow recipes at your disposal. Neither is more classic—they are just different approaches. Success with forming the chicks has everything to do with how carefully you pipe out the mixture. These candies must dry overnight, so plan accordingly.*

🍬 **LIFESPAN** *1 month at room temperature in airtight container in single layers*

Yield: *about 22 chicks*

Tools: *Pastry bag fitted with a ¹/₂-inch round tip, such as Ateco #806   Small soft artist's paintbrush*

INGREDIENTS

2 cups yellow colored sugar
9 tablespoons water
2¹/₂ teaspoons unflavored gelatin
1 cup granulated sugar

¹/₄ teaspoon yellow liquid coloring
1 tablespoon unsweetened Dutch-
   processed cocoa powder
Water

DIRECTIONS

1. Line a jelly-roll pan with aluminum foil. Sprinkle half of the colored sugar evenly over the pan.

2. Stir together 5 tablespoons of the water and the gelatin in a small bowl. Let sit 5 minutes to soften.

3. Meanwhile, stir remaining 4 table-spoons water and 1 cup granulated sugar together in a medium-size sauce-pan. Bring to a boil over medium-high heat and cook to 238°F (soft-ball stage). Remove from heat and whisk in gelatin mixture until dissolved.

4. Pour hot gelatin mixture into medium-size bowl and allow it to begin to cool, whisking occasionally to release heat. When it is just warm, begin to beat with an electric mixer on medium speed until the mixture turns opaque. Turn speed to high and beat until it is white, glossy, and forms soft peaks, about 10 minutes. Beat in food color-ing until color is evenly distributed.

5. Immediately scrape mixture into pastry bag fitted with a ¹/₂-inch round tip. Hold the pastry bag perpendicular to the prepared pan and just above the surface. Squeeze out marshmallow and allow it to form about a 1-inch-wide shape, then move the bag along the pan to form the body of the chick. It should be about 3 inches long,

tapering off as you go by easing up on the pressure. Finish with an upward motion to create a pointed "tail." The body shape should look like a teardrop with the pointed end curving up a bit.

6. Now place bag perpendicular and over the middle of the chick's body. Pipe marshmallow again, this time moving the bag toward the front of the chick, opposite the tail. When you get to the front of the chick's body, elevate the bag a little and pipe back along the portion you just piped, stop-ping before you get to the origination point of that layer and quickly bringing the tip over the top to form the head and face. This is best done by bringing the tip up, forward, and a bit down-ward, easing the pressure on the bag and finishing the "beak" off with a point (see photo).

7. Immediately sprinkle with remaining colored sugar while marshmallow is still moist. Place cocoa powder in a small bowl and stir in enough hot tap water with a spoon to make a thick but fluid cocoa "paint." Use artist's brush to dot small "eyes" on chicks, using photo for guidance. Allow chicks to dry overnight, uncovered, at room temperature. At this point they may be picked up and rolled in additional colored sugar to coat completely.

Solid Chocolate Bunnies

HOLIDAY *Easter*

TYPE *Molded candy*   **HABITAT** *Germany and United States*

DESCRIPTION *Solid chocolate Easter bunnies—simple as that. You may choose semisweet, milk, or white chocolate according to your preference.*

FIELD NOTES *Rabbits as fertility symbols hail back to pre-Christian days. The prolific rabbit was associated with reproduction and birth, and therefore with rebirth and springtime. In Germany, writings going back to the 1500s connect the rabbit to Easter, and the first edible bunnies appeared there around 1800. German settlers brought the Easter bunny to the United States (originally to Pennsylvania Dutch country). Nowadays many American children equate a chocolate Easter bunny with the holiday. You will need bunny-shaped molds, either flat-backed or a more elaborate 3-D. My mold makes four 3-dimensional 3³/₄-inch-tall bunnies that contain 2¹/₂ ounces of chocolate each. This is a smallish bunny, but the larger bunnies can be difficult to mold—ears can break and air bubbles can wreak havoc—so stick with a smaller size, at least to start!*

LIFESPAN *1 month at room temperature*

Yield: *four 3 3/4-inch-tall bunnies*

Tools: *Tomric bunny mold #WB120 • 4 cellophane candy bags • 4 decorative twist ties or pieces of ribbon*

▶●◀ INGREDIENTS

12 ounces couverture semisweet, milk, or white chocolate (see page 10), finely chopped

▶●◀ DIRECTIONS

1. If using a 3-D mold, assemble according to manufacturer's instructions. If using a flat mold, it is ready to use as is. Wipe the mold with a clean soft dishcloth to remove any dust.

2. Temper chocolate according to the directions on page 14. Slowly pour chocolate through bottom of mold for a 3-D mold, or straight into flat mold. Either way, bring chocolate all the way up to the very top of the mold's opening. Wipe off excess with a bench scraper or offset spatula. Allow to cool at cool room temperature until chocolate begins to firm, then refrigerate until completely hardened.

3. To unmold a 3-D mold, remove clips and/or separate the two halves, popping out the bunny. For a flat mold, place a flat plate on top of the back of the bunny and invert. You should be able to gently lift the mold off. If necessary, give the mold a slight twisting action.

4. Fingerprints will show up on the bunny, so handle him by the edges. (Professionals wear white cotton gloves.) If there are any unsightly seams, trim them away with a sharp knife. Place each bunny in a cellophane bag and close up the top to keep him safe—until you eat him!

Candy Tidbits

To give these little rabbits a custom look, you can use a contrasting color of chocolate to detail the eyes. For instance, for semisweet chocolate bunnies, melt some white chocolate and use a small, fine artist's brush to place a dot of white chocolate over the eye area. Refrigerate until set.

Easter Cream Eggs

HOLIDAY *Easter*

TYPE *Molded candy*   **HABITAT** *United States*

DESCRIPTION *These whimsical candies look like chocolate eggs on the outside, but when you bite into one, you will find a soft "white" and "yolk" of an egg—all sugar and deliciously edible, of course.*

FIELD NOTES *Every Easter season, the Cadbury Creme Egg commercials appear on TV. These homemade versions are not quite as gooey, but the effect is no less entrancing. Kids love these both for their super sweetness as well as their appearance. You can find the yellow food coloring in many crafts stores that have a cake-decorating section or order it from Wilton (see Resources). By melting the chocolate with shortening (do not substitute butter), you can avoid tempering.*

LIFESPAN *2 weeks refrigerated in airtight container in single layers separated by waxed or parchment paper*

Yield: *16 eggs*

INGREDIENTS

¹/₂ cup (1 stick) unsalted butter, at room
  temperature, cut into pieces
1¹/₂ teaspoons vanilla extract
¹/₂ teaspoon salt
²/₃ cup sweetened condensed milk

5 to 6 cups confectioners' sugar
Wilton Golden Yellow paste food coloring
8 ounces couverture semisweet chocolate
  (see page 10), finely chopped
2 teaspoons shortening

DIRECTIONS

1. Line a jelly-roll pan with aluminum foil, smoothing out any wrinkles. Coat foil with nonstick cooking spray.

2. In a large bowl with an electric mixer on medium speed, beat butter, vanilla, salt, and condensed milk until creamy, about 2 minutes. Add 5 cups confectioners' sugar and continue beating until creamy, smooth, and just stiff enough to knead by hand. Add more confectioners' sugar if necessary.

3. Remove about ³/₄ of the mixture to another bowl (measure this by eye). To remaining mixture, add half a pea-size dollop of yellow coloring and beat until incorporated and the mixture is a deep golden yellow color.

4. Dust your work surface with confectioners' sugar and knead both colors, separately, until smooth and pliable. Divide yellow and white mixtures into 16 portions each. Roll yellow pieces into small balls and white pieces into large balls. Flatten white balls with your palms and fingers and wrap them around yellow balls. Form into an egg shape and place on prepared pan. Refrigerate until very firm, about 1 hour.

5. Meanwhile, melt chocolate with shortening in a double boiler or microwave (or temper without shortening according to the directions on page 14). One by one, drop eggs into chocolate and use two large soup spoons to gently toss them back and forth until completely coated. Allow excess chocolate to drip back into the pot. Place eggs back on the pan. Refrigerate until firm.

Candy Tidbits

You could wrap these individually in large pieces of colored foil and place them in your Easter baskets.

Easter Egg with a Surprise

๑●๕ **HOLIDAY** *Easter*

๑●๕ **TYPE** *Molded candy*   ๑●๕ **HABITAT** *United States*

๑●๕ **DESCRIPTION** *These are large hollow Easter eggs, in your choice of chocolate, which you can fill with any small candy of your choosing, such as jelly beans or smaller chocolate eggs wrapped in foil. You could even put an Easter Peeper (page 64) inside!*

๑●๕ **FIELD NOTES** *You can choose whatever size egg that you like, but I have chosen one that is large enough to easily fill with additional candies. Other sizes would use different amounts of chocolate. A professional chocolatier would have metal bars (often used in candy making to mark out shapes on a flat pan) to prop the molds while they cool. I have suggested saucers or small plates, as those are probably easily accessible. The Tomric molds will have lips surrounding the mold, which can be placed on the saucers, allowing the egg portion of the mold to be suspended in between the little dishes and over the foil. The amount of chocolate is generous because it is helpful, when hollow molding, to have more rather than less.*

๑●๕ **LIFESPAN** *1 month refrigerated in airtight container*

Yield: *1 hollow egg*

Tools: *1 hollow egg mold, such as Tomric #H-824 (about 4 inches long x 3 inches wide)*
• *4 small saucers or plates* • *2 feet of ³/₈- or ¹/₂-inch ribbon, such as satin or grosgrain*

❧ INGREDIENTS

10 ounces couverture semisweet, milk, or
white chocolate (see page 10)

¹/₂ cup small candies, such as jelly beans or
tiny foil-wrapped chocolate eggs

❧ DIRECTIONS

1. Spread three large pieces of aluminum foil on counter. Wipe the mold with a clean soft dishcloth to remove any dust.

2. Temper chocolate according to the directions on page 14. Pour about one-third of tempered chocolate into half of the egg mold. Tilt to coat mold completely. Turn mold upside down and allow any excess to drip back into pot.

3. Hold mold, open side facing down, over one piece of foil and vigorously move mold in a circular motion. Any remaining excess chocolate will come out onto the foil.

4. Place egg, open side facing down, propped between the two saucers over second piece of foil. Allow to cool at cool room temperature.

5. Repeat steps 2 through 4 with other half of egg mold. The chocolate setting time may be aided by a brief stint in the refrigerator. Once chocolate has partially hardened, use the edge of a bench scraper to remove any excess chocolate from around the edges of the egg. Once chocolate is completely set you may build up additional coats of chocolate to make an egg with a thicker wall, if desired. You will know that the chocolate has completely set when you look at the domed sides of the molds and they look a bit cloudy. This means that the chocolate has

shrunk a bit on setting and pulled away from the surface of the mold.

6. To unmold, invert molds over a clean piece of aluminum foil. If chocolate does not come out easily, very gently twist the molds. You can also insert the tip of a small, thin knife along the edge of the egg and pry it away from the mold a little bit before inverting. If chocolate still won't come out, chill it further and repeat unmolding procedure.

7. To seal egg halves, reheat leftover chocolate until melted. Scrape into a zipper-lock plastic bag and snip a small hole in a bottom corner of the bag. Pour the small candies into one egg half; pipe a little melted chocolate onto the rim of that egg half, taking care not to allow any to drip over onto sides. Press the two halves together. Chill until seal is firm, about 1 hour.

8. Tie ribbon around the seam to camouflage it, making a pretty bow on top.

Candy Tidbits

You may decorate the egg further if you like. For instance, royal icing from the panoramic egg, page 74, or additional melted chocolate may be used to pipe decorations along the seam and on the domed portions of the egg. Chocolatiers wear white cotton gloves to avoid leaving fingerprints on the chocolate—and you can too. They are available through Sweet Celebrations (see Resources).

Easy Easter Nests with "Eggs"

🍬 **HOLIDAY** *Easter*

🍬 **TYPE** *Hand-formed candy*   🍬 **HABITAT** *United States*

🍬 **DESCRIPTION** *Crunchy chow mein noodles are covered with dark chocolate to resemble twigs and are formed into small nest shapes. Tiny jelly beans, the "eggs," fill the center.*

🍬 **FIELD NOTES** *These are so easy that I almost didn't include the recipe. But Easter is a very family-oriented holiday and I wanted to include a super-easy, kid-friendly candy that you could make with even very young children. Make as many as you have guests and place them on plates as a table favor. The kids will be able to say, "I made them!" The recipe can easily be doubled, tripled, or quadrupled.*

🍬 **LIFESPAN** *1 week refrigerated in airtight container in single layers separated by waxed or parchment paper*

Yield: *7 nests*

❧●❧ INGREDIENTS

10 ounces semisweet chocolate, finely
chopped
2¹/₂ cups chow mein noodles
(one 5-ounce can)

¹/₄ cup small jelly beans or candy-coated
chocolate eggs

❧●❧ DIRECTIONS

1. Line a jelly-roll pan with aluminum
   foil, smoothing out any wrinkles. Coat
   foil with nonstick cooking spray.

2. Melt chocolate in a double boiler or in
   a large bowl in the microwave.

3. Very gently fold chow mein noodles
   into chocolate, taking care not to break
   them, as the longer lengths are what
   give you that "twig" look.

4. Spoon 7 mounds out onto the prepared
   pan and use your fingers to form a nest
   shape about 4 inches across. Make a
   depression in the center.

5. Refrigerate to set chocolate completely,
   about 30 minutes. Sprinkle a few jelly
   beans in the center of each nest before
   serving.

**Candy
Tidbits**

Milk chocolate looks great
too, and you could also use
small speckled malted-milk
candy eggs for a more
realistic approach.

Panoramic Sugar Egg

🍬 **HOLIDAY** *Easter*

🍬 **TYPE** *Molded candy*   🍬 **HABITAT** *United States*

🍬 **DESCRIPTION** *While this is theoretically edible, it may be more fun to just look at, as it is designed to delight the eye. (And because it is a lot of work, you may not want it to be gobbled up!) This recipe features an egg filled with a little pastoral Easter scene.*

🍬 **FIELD NOTES** *No getting around it . . . this is captivating, but quite a bit of work. It's a project that takes time, patience, and some amount of dexterity. While older children can help with the whole recipe, it might be better to bring the younger set in at the end for the decoration. I highly recommend that you use Wilton's Petite Sugar Egg Kit (see Resources), which will give you most of what you need. The set comes with directions; I have taken some liberty and attempted to simplify the process for you somewhat, but I have written this recipe assuming that you will be using the kit.*

🍬 **LIFESPAN** *1 year at room temperature in airtight container*

Yield: *1 gorgeous egg*

Tools: *1 Wilton Petite Sugar Egg Kit (egg molds, decorating tips, decorating bags, meringue powder, food coloring, and icing decorations) Cornstarch Icing spatula Two 6-inch cardboard rounds Toothpick Sandpaper or microplane grater 2 couplers Shallow basket Eye dropper*

●◄ INGREDIENTS

For the egg:
2 cups superfine granulated sugar
4 teaspoons water
1/2 teaspoon meringue powder
  (from the kit)

For the royal icing:
2 cups confectioners' sugar, sifted
1 tablespoon plus 1 teaspoon meringue
  powder (from the kit)
2 to 3 tablespoons water

●◄ DIRECTIONS

1. Unpack egg kit. Wipe both egg halves with a clean soft dishcloth to make sure they are dust free. Place about 1 tablespoon of cornstarch in one egg half. Seal with other egg half and shake to lightly coat the insides of the egg. It might not look like it is coating the surface, but it is. Open the egg and shake out excess cornstarch.

2. Place superfine sugar and 1/2 teaspoon meringue powder (from the kit) in a medium-size mixing bowl. Place water in a small cup and, using eye dropper, add 5 drops of yellow liquid food coloring (from the kit) and stir to combine. Add colored water to sugar and whisk until completely combined. You might need to finish off the mixing by using your hands. The mixture should be a solid yellow color throughout and the texture of wet sand. Squeeze it in your palm; it should hold together.

3. Pack sugar into both egg halves, pressing down firmly with fingers and palms. This is very important, so don't skimp with the elbow grease. You want it firmly packed right up

to the top and even a little above. Use a bench scraper or icing spatula to level off the top, using the edges of the egg as a guide. The edges should be as perfect as possible. Sprinkle a little bit of cornstarch on top of each flat egg surface.

4. Place a cardboard round over one of the eggs, and, holding both egg and cardboard, flip egg over. The cardboard should now be on the bottom. Place on table and gently remove egg mold. It should release easily. If it

Candy Tidbits

You can tailor the egg to your liking. Make the egg light blue with blue food coloring; the white clouds will look gorgeous! Make the egg horizontal by slicing off the bottom from the long side. Use the tips to pipe different shapes, or make fancier frosting decorations by using your own tips.

does not, tap the rounded side of the egg mold with handle of bench scraper or icing spatula and try again. Repeat with second egg.

5. One egg will be rounded. The other one will have a flat area, which will be where the cut-out window will be. First you have to form the bottoms of the eggs so that they have a flat base upon which to stand. Use an icing spatula to slice off the bottom ¼ inch from each broader rounded end. You can do this by eye because any imperfections can be fixed with sandpaper after the egg is dry.

6. To make the window, use a toothpick to dot a larger oval around the flat area approximately 1 inch beyond the flat area's border. Use icing spatula to horizontally slice through the egg, about ½ inch from the top, so that it bisects these markings, but leave the top portion in place—do not remove.

7. Allow the eggs to dry at room temperature at least 1½ hours or up to 4 hours. It all depends on the ambient humidity. The next step is to hollow out the eggs, and the outside of the eggs must have developed a dry shell in order to do this successfully. Gently touch the outside of the eggs. They should be dry, and if you press very gently they should feel hard and crusty.

8. Preheat oven to 200°F. Line a jelly-roll pan with parchment paper; set aside. First hollow out the egg with the window. Use icing spatula to remove the portion that you sliced off before but didn't remove. Use icing spatula to lift the portion up and off; discard. The sugar beneath will be soft. Use toothpick to dot an oval ¼ inch inside this oval window border. Use a teaspoon to begin scooping out some of the center, but don't try to scoop all the way through. Very, very carefully turn egg over and begin scooping from

that side, leaving a ¼-inch-thick shell/border all around. It is very easy to break the egg at this point, so take your time.

9. To hollow out other half, mark with toothpick ¼ inch from edge of flat side and scoop out egg to leave it evenly concave with a ¼-inch-thick shell all around.

10. *Important:* If at any time you break the egg, you can reuse soft sugar to begin again. In other words, you can recoup to some degree, but you will have lost a lot of time. Be very careful during the scooping procedure.

11. Place eggs on prepared pan and bake for about 25 minutes or until bone dry. Place pan on rack; do not touch eggs yet. Allow to cool completely.

12. Now assess whether edges need any help. Stand both eggs up on their blunt ends. They should be sturdy (with flat bottoms) and level. If they are not, sand areas that might need to be removed. The best technique is to place sandpaper flat on the table and to rub the egg surface over it gently and lightly. A microplane grater can be rubbed over any spots as well to remove parts that protrude.

13. To make royal icing, place all icing ingredients, using 2 tablespoons water, in a medium-size bowl and beat with an electric mixer until light and fluffy, scraping down bowl once or twice, about 2 minutes. Remove about one-third of the icing to another bowl; tint this icing dark green using liquid coloring; it should be a good color to mimic grass. Leave larger portion white. Cover bowls with clean, damp cloths to keep icing from drying out.

14. Insert coupler in decorator bag and affix tip #3. Fill with white icing. Pipe clouds along upper concave area of egg half (see photo to mimic piping).

Insert coupler in second decorator bag, affix tip #16, and fill with green icing. Pipe shells inside the bottom of the same egg half, going all the way to the back and up part of the back wall and coming all the way to the front to mimic grass. Nestle sugar chick and egg decorations (that come with the kit) in the "grass" (see photo).

15. Remove tips from couplers, wash them well, and attach them to opposite colored bags (the #3 tip should be with the green icing and #16 with the white). Wrap plastic wrap around #3 tip to keep it moist, as it will sit for a while.

16. Pipe a line of white icing along outer edge of back half and larger rim of egg with window. Gently press these edges together and stand egg upright. Wrap a piece of plastic wrap around tip opening to keep icing from forming a crust. Allow egg to dry at least 1 hour. Use same bag and tip to pipe a shell border around seam of egg (see photo for details) and edge of window. Place flowers (from the kit) on top/side edge of egg for décor (see photo). Using green icing and #3 tip, pipe small leaf shapes here and there among flowers. Allow egg to dry.

Candy Tidbits

If you'd like to nest your egg in a basket with coconut "grass," place 3 cups sweetened flaked coconut in small mixing bowl. Add about 10 drops green food coloring. Toss with a fork until color is distributed evenly. Place this "grass" in basket. When egg is dry, nestle it in the "grass" to display.

Matzoh Brown Sugar Buttercrunch

≫●≪ HOLIDAY *Passover*

≫●≪ TYPE *Bark-type candy*   **≫●≪ HABITAT** *United States*

≫●≪ DESCRIPTION *Did the title catch your eye? Yes, matzoh crackers are the base for this very easy and tasty confection. The matzoh are simply covered with a brown sugar–butter mixture, baked until bubbly, and then slathered with a melted chocolate layer.*

≫●≪ FIELD NOTES *While I was searching for a Passover treat, all of a sudden friends and family were referring to a confection similar to this one. The first mention came from a reference librarian at my local library—which just served to remind me that whatever question you may have, ask it of your reference librarian! They are a fantastic resource and you will be continually amazed at the depth and breadth of their knowledge.*

≫●≪ LIFESPAN *1 month refrigerated in airtight container in single layers separated by waxed or parchment paper*

Yield: *about 1 1/2 pounds buttercrunch to yield about 18 servings*

INGREDIENTS

5 whole lightly salted matzohs (about 7 x 7 1/2 inches)

1 cup (2 sticks) unsalted butter, cut into pieces

1 cup light brown sugar

8 ounces semisweet chocolate, finely chopped

DIRECTIONS

1. Preheat oven to 350°F. Coat a jelly-roll pan with nonstick cooking spray. Place matzohs side by side in pan, breaking them to fit so that the entire surface of the pan is covered.

2. Cook butter and sugar in a small saucepan over medium heat, stirring often, until butter melts. Bring to a simmer, and simmer mixture for 5 minutes.

3. Immediately pour brown sugar mixture over matzohs, covering them completely. Spread mixture around with an offset spatula if necessary.

4. Bake for about 12 minutes or until bubbly and edges are starting to turn golden brown. Remove from oven and place on cooling rack.

5. Immediately sprinkle chocolate over surface of matzohs. Let sit for about 3 minutes or until chocolate has softened, then spread chocolate all over surface with an offset spatula. Chill until chocolate firms, about 30 minutes. Break into pieces.

Candy Tidbits

Feel free to use milk chocolate instead of semisweet. (White chocolate might be a bit too sweet, but go for it if you like it!) You can also sprinkle the still-wet chocolate with chopped nuts or coconut.

Licorice Toffee

🍬 **HOLIDAY** *National Licorice Day*

🍬 **TYPE** *Poured candy*   🍬 **HABITAT** *United States*

🍬 **DESCRIPTION** *These are chewy, toffee-like candies with the distinctive licorice flavor that comes from anise.*

🍬 **FIELD NOTES** *I was looking for a good reason to include a recipe for licorice, and, lo and behold, according to the National Confectioners Association and its Web site, www.candyusa.org, April 12 is indeed National Licorice Day! A friend gave me this recipe, but her version called for anise extract; I prefer the potent, pure flavor of anise oil (try LorAnn's). This candy does have a tendency to stick to the bottom of the pan, so follow the instructions faithfully.*

🍬 **LIFESPAN** *2 weeks at room temperature in airtight container*

Yield: *64 toffees*

⊱●⊰ INGREDIENTS

1 cup (2 sticks) unsalted butter, at room
temperature, cut into pieces
2 cups granulated sugar
One 14-ounce can sweetened condensed
milk
1 cup light corn syrup

Pinch of salt
1 teaspoon anise oil
$^1/_2$ teaspoon Wilton black paste food
coloring
64 small square candy wrappers or
cellophane

⊱●⊰ DIRECTIONS

1. Line a 9-inch square baking pan with
aluminum foil so that foil overhangs
by a few inches on all sides. Smooth
out any wrinkles, and butter foil
generously.

2. Melt butter in a medium-size deep
saucepan over medium heat. Quickly
stir in sugar, milk, corn syrup, and salt
until combined.

3. Continue to cook until mixture
reaches 245°F (firm-ball stage).
Immediately remove from heat,
add anise oil and coloring, and
stir to combine. Quickly pour

into prepared pan and place on rack
to cool completely, about 4 hours or
overnight. Unmold by pulling foil up
and out of pan; peel off foil.

4. Cut into 64 squares (8 x 8) using an
oiled bench scraper and wrap individually in wrappers or cellophane.

Candy Tidbits

I always feel a little odd using
black food coloring and do not use
it very often. The trick when using it is
to use enough. Too little and the toffee
will be a very unappetizing brownish-
gray color. We expect licorice to
be black, so it is actually more
appealing to make it a true
black color.

Crystallized Flowers

❦ **HOLIDAY** *Summer solstice, birthdays*

. . . .

❦ **TYPE** *Hand-formed candy*   ❦ **HABITAT** *United States and Europe*

. . . .

❦ **DESCRIPTION** *How can you improve upon nature's perfection? In this case, with edible flowers, you add a little bit of sugar to crystallize them. After they have dried, they will be crisp and crystalline, and very elegant.*

. . . .

❦ **FIELD NOTES** *Crystallized flowers are used throughout the world to decorate cakes and other pastries. The reason I associate these with birthdays is that you can make them ahead and have them ready anytime to decorate a birthday cake or cupcakes, making the dessert extra-special. I used a pansy in the photo, but other edible flowers can be used, such as small roses (or individual rose petals), violets, nasturtiums, or violas. Many flowers, such as tulips, are edible but not necessarily delicious. To start, stick with those I mention. Also, make sure to purchase superfine sugar, which has a lovely crystalline quality. Note that these must dry overnight.*

. . . .

❦ **LIFESPAN** *1 month at room temperature in airtight container in single layer*

Yield: *24 flowers*

Tools: *Tweezers • Small soft artist's paintbrush*

❖ INGREDIENTS

24 small (I to 2 inches in diameter) edible flowers such as unsprayed pansies or roses, leaves and stems removed

2 cups superfine sugar
2 large egg whites

❖ DIRECTIONS

1. Make sure flowers are dry. You want perfect blooms without any blemishes, nicks, or cuts.

2. Place sugar in a small bowl. Whisk egg whites until frothy in another small bowl.

3. Hold the base of a flower with tweezers or your fingertips. Use the brush to coat every surface of the petals with a thin, even coat of egg white. Make sure to thoroughly coat the petals, as you cannot successfully go back and patch up after the sugar is applied.

4. Hold flower over the bowl of sugar. Use a teaspoon to scoop up the sugar and sprinkle it evenly over flower. Shake flower gently to see if any areas still need sugar, and sprinkle sugar where needed.

5. Place flower on cooling rack to dry. Repeat with other flowers. They should dry at least overnight, or until completely dry and crisp.

Candy Tidbits

A Blue Magic device (see Resources) is very helpful in keeping these flowers super dry. Just place one in the airtight container along with the flowers.

Pumpkin Candy
(Docinhos de Abóbora)

⇒●⇐ **HOLIDAY** *St. John's Day*

⇒●⇐ **TYPE** *Hand-formed candy*   ⇒●⇐ **HABITAT** *Brazil*

⇒●⇐ **DESCRIPTION** *This pumpkin candy also features coconut. It is rich and easy to make.*

⇒●⇐ **FIELD NOTES** *St. John is the saint to whom young women look for help in finding a spouse. St. John's Day falls on June 24, which is the coldest part of the year in Brazil. It is a very festive day, with lanterns hung and bonfires burning. Corn and sweet potatoes are used in many holiday dishes. Pumpkin, being a large crop as well, is prepared in various forms, such as these candies, and served to friends and family. Because they are fairly sweet, I have added lemon zest to the classic recipe to temper the sweetness somewhat.*

⇒●⇐ **LIFESPAN** *1 month refrigerated in airtight container in single layers separated by waxed or parchment paper*

Yield: *about 60 balls*

ᐱ●ᐊ INGREDIENTS

1 cup granulated sugar
$^1/_2$ cup water
1 cup canned pumpkin
2 cups unsweetened grated coconut

1 cup sweetened flaked coconut
1 teaspoon lemon zest
60 small fluted paper cups

ᐱ●ᐊ DIRECTIONS

1. Stir sugar and water together in a medium-size saucepan. Bring to a boil over medium-high heat and cook to 235°F (soft-ball stage).

2. Whisk in pumpkin, coconuts, and lemon zest. Continue to cook over medium-high heat, stirring almost constantly to prevent burning. The mixture will be very thick, but just keep stirring it. The pumpkin will become somewhat translucent and the mixture will dry out completely, about 10 minutes.

Scrape into shallow bowl and allow to cool to room temperature, then refrigerate until chilled and firm, about 6 hours or overnight.

3. Roll mixture into 1-inch balls and place in paper cups.

Candy Tidbits

If you would like to make these fancier looking, you can roll them in granulated sugar or extra coconut. You could even toast coconut and give them a roll around in that.

Classic Creamy Fudge

>●< **HOLIDAY** *Fourth of July*

>●< **TYPE** *Bar candy*   >●< **HABITAT** *United States*

>●< **DESCRIPTION** *At its best, fudge is creamy, sweet, dense, and rich. This classic recipe, which requires a thermometer—and lots of bicep-straining beating—has a very creamy texture, if it doesn't turn grainy, which can happen even to experienced candy makers. Dry weather makes the outcome more reliable, as does the addition of corn syrup. Some classic versions use cocoa powder instead of chocolate, sweetened chocolate instead of unsweetened, and milk products ranging from skim milk to heavy cream. This recipe is somewhat less sweet due to the unsweetened chocolate, and it is of medium richness due to the blend of milk and cream.*

>●< **FIELD NOTES** *I associate fudge with summer vacation. It seems as though most vacation spots have an old-fashioned candy store that kids of all ages will find one way or another. The history of fudge is sketchy but appears to be attached to many different women's colleges from the first half of the 1900s. It seems as though Smith, Vassar, and Wellesley Colleges all had their share of coeds whipping up batches in their dorm rooms—that's one way to ease the stress of exams!*

>●< **LIFESPAN** *2 weeks refrigerated in airtight container in single layers separated by waxed or parchment paper*

Yield: *64 fudge squares*

✥●✥ INGREDIENTS

2 cups granulated sugar
1/2 cup heavy cream
1/4 cup whole milk
3 tablespoons light corn syrup
4 ounces unsweetened chocolate, finely chopped

2 tablespoons unsalted butter, cut into small pieces
1 1/2 teaspoons vanilla extract
1 cup toasted walnut halves (see page 16), coarsely chopped

✥●✥ DIRECTIONS

1. Thoroughly coat all inside surfaces of an 8-inch square baking pan with non-stick cooking spray.

2. In a large nonreactive pot, stir together granulated sugar, cream, milk, and corn syrup. Heat over medium heat until it comes to a simmer; simmer for 1 minute.

3. Stir in chopped chocolate, cover, and simmer for 1 minute—do not stir from this point on or you will encourage graininess. The cover will redirect any steam downward, which will help wash down any sugar crystals clinging to the sides of the pot.

4. Uncover and simmer until mixture reaches 238°F (soft-ball stage), about 10 minutes. Remove from heat and scatter butter pieces on surface without disturbing fudge. Allow to sit until temperature comes down to 110°F, about 30 minutes.

5. Pour vanilla extract over fudge. If you are feeling strong, grab a wooden spoon and vigorously beat fudge using broad strokes, or scrape fudge into the bowl of a stand mixer fitted with a paddle attachment and beat on medium speed. Either way, beat until mixture *just* loses its sheen. Quickly fold in nuts and scrape mixture into prepared pan. Use a rubber spatula or your fingers to coax fudge into corners and into an even layer.

6. Let fudge sit at room temperature for 1 hour. Cover with plastic wrap and refrigerate overnight before cutting and serving. Cut into 64 squares (8 x 8).

Pecan Penuche

≫●≪ **HOLIDAY** *Fourth of July*

≫●≪ **TYPE** *Bar candy*   ≫●≪ **HABITAT** *United States*

≫●≪ **DESCRIPTION** *Penuche is simply a brown sugar fudge—no chocolate here. The blend of dark and light brown sugars yields a deep, rich taste. Toasted pecans enhance the brown sugar flavor, but feel free to try walnuts instead. As with all classic fudge-type candies, remember that a thermometer is helpful and humidity can wreak havoc—save this recipe for a dry day.*

≫●≪ **FIELD NOTES** *Penuche has been around for decades and is a very popular alternative to chocolate-based fudge. It is usually sold by the pound right alongside fudge in candy stores. The word* penuche *is most likely a derivation of a word for a Mexican style of brown sugar.*

≫●≪ **LIFESPAN** *2 weeks refrigerated in airtight container in single layers separated by waxed or parchment paper*

Yield: *64 penuche squares*

⇾●⇽ INGREDIENTS

1 1/2 cups granulated sugar
1/2 cup packed dark brown sugar
1/2 cup packed light brown sugar
1/3 cup whole milk
1/3 cup heavy cream

2 tablespoons unsalted butter, cut into small pieces
1 teaspoon vanilla extract
3/4 cup toasted pecan halves (see page 16), coarsely chopped

⇾●⇽ DIRECTIONS

1. Thoroughly coat all inside surfaces of an 8-inch square baking pan with non-stick cooking spray.

2. In a large nonreactive pot, stir together all three sugars, milk, and cream. Cook over medium heat until it comes to a simmer; cover and simmer for 1 minute—do not stir from this point on or you will encourage graininess. The cover will redirect any steam downward, which will help wash down any sugar crystals clinging to the sides of the pot.

3. Uncover and simmer until mixture reaches 238°F (soft-ball stage), about 10 minutes. Remove from heat and scatter butter pieces on surface without disturbing penuche. Allow to sit until temperature comes down to 110°F, about 30 minutes.

4. Pour vanilla extract over fudge. If you are feeling strong, grab a wooden spoon and vigorously beat penuche using broad strokes, or scrape penuche into the bowl of a stand mixer fitted with a paddle attachment and beat on medium speed. Either way, beat until mixture *just* loses its sheen. Quickly fold in nuts and scrape mixture into prepared pan. Use a rubber spatula or your fingers to coax penuche into corners and into an even layer.

5. Let penuche sit at room temperature for 1 hour. Cover with plastic wrap and refrigerate overnight before cutting and serving. Cut into 64 squares (8 x 8).

Easiest Fudge in the World

🍬 HOLIDAY *Fourth of July*

🍬 TYPE *Bar candy*   **🍬 HABITAT** *United States*

🍬 DESCRIPTION *This fudge is so easy and so foolproof that even if you have never made candy before, I guarantee great results! How can you pass that up? The chocolate combines with the sweetened condensed milk to make a creamy fudge that also just happens to be very quick to prepare.*

🍬 FIELD NOTES *I have given you a very basic recipe along with several variations (see Candy Tidbits) and you may think of more yourself.*

🍬 LIFESPAN *2 weeks refrigerated in airtight container in single layers separated by waxed or parchment paper*

Yield: *40 large fudge squares*

❧●❧ INGREDIENTS

2 pounds bittersweet or semisweet chocolate, finely chopped

4 tablespoons (¹/₂ stick) unsalted butter, cut into pieces

Two 14-ounce cans sweetened condensed milk

1 teaspoon vanilla extract

❧●❧ DIRECTIONS

1. Thoroughly coat all inside surfaces of a 9 x 13-inch baking pan with nonstick cooking spray.

2. Melt chocolate and butter in a double boiler or in a large bowl in the microwave, stirring until smooth. Remove from heat and stir in condensed milk and vanilla extract. The mixture should be completely smooth.

3. Scrape fudge into prepared pan. Use a rubber spatula or your fingers to coax fudge into corners and into an even layer.

4. Refrigerate 2 hours or until firm enough to cut. Cut into 40 squares (8 x 5).

Candy Tidbits

For Rocky Road Fudge, add 1¹/₂ cups miniature marshmallows and 1¹/₂ cups chopped toasted walnuts or pecans to fudge before scraping into pan. For Chunky Fudge, add 1¹/₂ cups dark raisins and 1 cup chopped toasted peanuts. For Fudge X 3, divide recipe in half. Use bittersweet chocolate for one half and spread in pan. Use milk chocolate for second half and spread in pan on top of first half. While still soft, scatter 1 cup miniature semisweet chocolate chips on top and press into surface with your fingers.

Saltwater Taffy

>●< HOLIDAY *Fourth of July*

>●< TYPE *Pulled candy*   **>●< HABITAT** *United States*

>●< DESCRIPTION *Okay, just a friendly warning here: I take no responsibility for any damaged dental work! That is what I actually told my recipe testers. Taffy, any taffy, is by its very nature an extremely chewy candy. Here I have made a simple vanilla flavor. At first the nugget feels rather firm, even hard, in your mouth. If it is very humid, it might be soft right away, but don't bet on it. Then your body temperature starts to soften the taffy as you chew and it becomes chewy, very chewy! Enjoy, but please be careful. Avoid this recipe if you wear braces or have any loose fillings!*

>●< FIELD NOTES *Saltwater taffy doesn't require real salt water from the ocean. The origin of the name is blurry. Taffy was offered at country fairs in the Midwest by the 1880s, and sometime during that decade it appeared in Atlantic City as "saltwater" taffy. Today, particularly at seaside resorts, you will find candy stores offering dozens of flavors, from vanilla to root beer, cherry, and mint.*

>●< LIFESPAN *1 month at room temperature in airtight container*

Yield: *about 50 candies*

Tools: *Scissors • 50 small square candy wrappers or cellophane*

▷●◁ INGREDIENTS

1½ cups granulated sugar
2 tablespoons cornstarch
½ cup water
½ cup light corn syrup
½ teaspoon salt

2 tablespoons unsalted butter, cut into
  4 pieces
½ teaspoon vanilla extract or flavoring of
  choice
Liquid food coloring (optional)

▷●◁ DIRECTIONS

1. Lightly oil the entire surface of a jelly-roll pan with canola oil. Lightly oil a pair of scissors.

2. Whisk sugar and cornstarch together in a medium-size saucepan. Gradually stir water into mixture, then stir in corn syrup, salt, and butter.

3. Cook over medium heat, stirring occasionally, until sugar dissolves, then cease stirring and boil over high heat until it reaches 260°F (hard-ball stage). Remove from heat and stir in vanilla and food coloring, if using.

4. Scrape mixture onto prepared pan and set on rack to cool, about 20 minutes. During that time, occasionally scrape the edges up with a bench scraper, folding them over the middle. You just want to move it around a little and release any heat from underneath.

5. When the taffy is just warm and you are able to handle it, lightly oil your hands, pick up the taffy, and start to pull. Gather it together and pull, gather and pull. It will become more opaque and develop a satiny finish. Keep pulling until it starts to get firm, about 5 minutes of continuous pulling (but it depends on the room temperature and temperature of the candy).

6. Quickly pull taffy into ropes about ½ inch wide and cut 1-inch lengths with oiled scissors. Place pieces back on pan and allow to cool. Wrap individually when completely cooled.

Candy Tidbits

Here the flavor variations are endless. Try some cherry flavoring and a few drops of red food coloring; lime or sour apple flavoring with green coloring; lemon with yellow . . . you get the gist. The amount of flavor and color can be adjusted as desired. Also, flavorings will vary by brand, so start out with a smaller amount, taste, and adjust.

Molasses Taffy

🍬 **HOLIDAY** *Fourth of July*

🍬 **TYPE** *Pulled candy*   🍬 **HABITAT** *United States*

🍬 **DESCRIPTION** *This chewy confection is full of deep, rich molasses flavor. It might not appeal to kids, but it is great candy that is not over-the-top sugary sweet.*

🍬 **FIELD NOTES** *Molasses taffy, and candies featuring molasses, are quite old-fashioned in that they were very popular before processed sugar was widely available and/or affordable.*

🍬 **LIFESPAN** *1 month at room temperature in airtight container*

Yield: *about 50 candies*

Tools: *Scissors • 50 small square candy wrappers or cellophane*

▷●◁ INGREDIENTS

1½ cups granulated sugar
1½ cups unsulfured molasses
⅔ cup water

¼ cup (½ stick) unsalted butter
½ teaspoon vanilla extract
⅛ teaspoon baking soda

▷●◁ DIRECTIONS

1. Lightly oil the entire surface of a jelly-roll pan with canola oil. Lightly oil a pair of scissors.

2. Stir sugar, molasses, and water together in a medium-size deep saucepan. Cook over medium heat, swirling pan occasionally, until it reaches 260°F (hard-ball stage). Watch carefully to prevent it from boiling over. Remove from heat and stir in butter, vanilla, and baking soda.

3. Immediately scrape mixture onto prepared pan and set on rack to cool, about 20 minutes. During that time, occasionally scrape the edges up with a bench scraper and fold them over the middle. You just want to move it around a little and release any heat from underneath.

4. When the taffy is just warm and you are able to handle it, lightly oil your hands, pick up the taffy, and start to pull. Gather it together and pull, gather and pull. It will become more opaque and develop a satiny finish. Keep pulling until it starts to firm up, about 5 minutes of continuous pulling (but it depends on the room temperature and temperature of the candy).

5. Quickly pull taffy into ropes about ½ inch wide and cut 1-inch lengths with the scissors. Place pieces back on pan and allow to cool. Wrap individually when completely cooled.

Candy Tidbits

Get your biceps ready for a workout. The final texture of any taffy depends on the pulling stage, which should be lengthy and thorough. That's why there used to be social events called "taffy pulls," where many strong arms would be on hand to help.

Sugar Sparklers

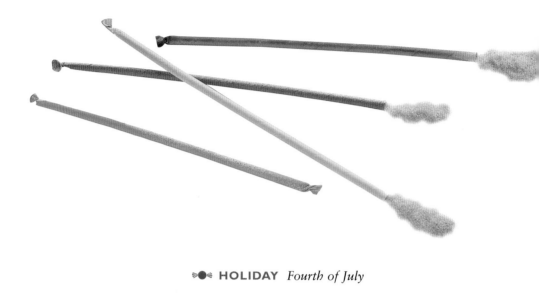

▸●◂ **HOLIDAY** *Fourth of July*

▸●◂ **TYPE** *Hand-formed candy*   ▸●◂ **HABITAT** *United States*

▸●◂ **DESCRIPTION** *Truth be told, these candies, sold as Pixy Stix in stores, are practically pure sugar, but if you are a candy lover, a little sugar is not going to scare you off. These have the fruity, sweet-tart flavor of the purchased kind. If you are not fond of really tart-sour candies, reduce the amount of citric acid. But kids seem to love that flavor, and they are usually the ones who eat these, rather than adults.*

▸●◂ **FIELD NOTES** *While researching this recipe, I was surprised to meet many people who didn't know what Pixy Stix were! They are paper or plastic straws filled with a sugary, granular candy. Kids open one end of the straw and pour the flavored sugar right into their mouths. These are super easy to make, but it takes some care to get the mixture into the straws. You must have a tiny funnel; the one I used was labeled as being for perfume and small bottles. The bottom opening was actually too small for the sugar mixture to flow through, so I cut it to be as large as possible but so that it would still fit in the straw. Citric acid can be mail ordered from Sweet Celebrations (see Resources).*

▸●◂ **LIFESPAN** *1 month at room temperature in airtight container*

Yield: *about 35 sparklers*

Tools: *One 2-cup Pyrex measuring cup • 2 cups dry rice, beans, or popcorn kernels • One 1-cup Pyrex measuring cup • Thirty-five 7¹/₂-inch paper or plastic straws • 1 very small funnel*

INGREDIENTS

6 tablespoons superfine granulated sugar
¹/₈ teaspoon citric acid

One 0.13-ounce package of Kool-Aid in any flavor of your choice

DIRECTIONS

1. Fill the 2-cup measuring cup with dry rice.

2. Place all the ingredients in the 1-cup measuring cup and whisk or stir to combine.

3. Twist one end of all the straws, about 1 inch from the end, to seal them as well as you can.

4. Place a straw in the rice, which will hold it still. Insert the funnel into open end of straw and scoop about ¹/₂ teaspoon of mixture into funnel. If the mixture does not flow through, use a teaspoon to gently tap the edge of the funnel so that the sugar mixture flows into the straw. Fill the

straw to within about 1 inch of the top. Twist the open end closed. Repeat process with remaining straws.

Candy Tidbits

If you can find paper straws, they are easier to twist shut and I recommend them, but they are very hard to locate. The plastic ones actually do twist and seal sufficiently. Or as an alternative to straws, you can use miniature baby bottles as a cutesy kid-friendly party favor. Wilton makes these (see Resources). The 4-inch-high bottles come with assorted pastel lids in packs of 6, and each holds a little more than 2 tablespoons of the sugar mixture, so you should double the recipe to be able to mostly fill the 6 bottles.

Mendiants

≋●≋ HOLIDAY *Autumnal equinox*

≋●≋ TYPE *Drop candy*   **≋●≋ HABITAT** *France*

≋●≋ DESCRIPTION *These are simply bite-size discs of chocolate topped with fruits, nuts, and cacao nibs.*

≋●≋ FIELD NOTES *These are quick and easy as well as elegant and are found in France's chocolate stores at any given time of year. The French word* mendiant *refers to beggars as well as those of monastic persuasion. The toppings on the chocolate represent four mendicant orders. The colors of the items are supposed to represent the colors of their various robes, but I have found different items mentioned. Most popular seem to be hazelnuts, figs, almonds, and raisins. I have chosen toppings for flavor, color, and shape and to give an autumnal feel, but you can use whatever you prefer. The cacao nibs are actual bits of cocoa bean. The ones I use are produced by Scharffen Berger and can be mail ordered through Sweet Celebrations (see Resources) and found at Whole Foods stores nationwide.*

≋●≋ LIFESPAN *1 month refrigerated in airtight container in single layers separated by waxed or parchment paper*

Yield: *36 rounds*

➤●◄ INGREDIENTS

22 unsalted roasted cashews
3 dried apricots
36 dried cranberries

8 ounces couverture bittersweet
chocolate (see page 10), finely chopped
1 teaspoon cacao nibs

➤●◄ DIRECTIONS

1. Line a jelly-roll pan with aluminum foil, shiny side up, smoothing out any wrinkles, or line the pan with a piece of acetate.

2. Split cashews in half lengthwise along seam. You need only 36 halves total, so you have extra in case of breakage.

3. Slice apricots into 6 slivers, then cut the slivers in half crosswise. The cranberries can stay as is, unless they are very large, in which case you should cut them in half (and you would then need half as many).

4. Temper chocolate according to the directions on page 14. Use a teaspoon to drop 1½-inch rounds of chocolate onto prepared pan. Space these rounds apart so that they are not touching. Drop about six cacao nibs onto each wet disc, clustered in one area, then place other toppings as shown in photo.

5. Chill until firm, about 30 minutes. Enjoy at room temperature.

Candy Tidbits

Here are some other toppings to try: candied ginger, dried cherries, golden raisins, and slivers of Brazil nuts.

Fruit and Nut–Stuffed Dates

HOLIDAY *Simchat Torah*

TYPE *Hand-formed candy*   **HABITAT** *Curaçao*

DESCRIPTION *This is a very simple confection to make. My version has a mixture of walnuts, apricots, and orange zest stuffed into dates. Similar confections, often with marzipan, are found in North Africa.*

FIELD NOTES *Simchat Torah is a floating October Jewish holiday that is defined as "rejoicing in the law" and concludes the annual reading of the Torah. There used to be a large population of Sephardic Jews on the island of Curaçao, dating back to the mid-1600s. Their numbers are now dwindling, but those who remain have a lively community. In fact, one of the synagogues is said to have more than a dozen Torah scrolls dating back over 300 years. This is a typical holiday recipe that would be offered to family and friends.*

LIFESPAN *1 month refrigerated in airtight container in single layers separated by waxed or parchment paper*

Yield: *24 dates*

⋙●⋘ INGREDIENTS

24 plump dates, such as Medjool
Heaping ¹/₂ cup finely chopped apricots
¹/₃ cup toasted walnut halves (see page
  16), finely chopped

3 tablespoons minced candied orange peel
1¹/₂ teaspoons orange zest
1 tablespoon sweet kosher wine or
  orange Curaçao liqueur (optional)

⋙●⋘ DIRECTIONS

1. Make a lengthwise slit in each date, making sure not to cut through the back/bottom of the date. Remove and discard pits, if there are any.

2. Stir together apricots, nuts, candied peel, and zest in a small bowl. Moisten with wine or liqueur, if desired. I find it best to mix everything together with my fingers, but a wooden spoon will also work.

3. Use a teaspoon to scoop and press a small amount of the mixture into each date. Use your fingers to make it look neat and attractive, and press the sides of the dates together around the filling, letting some of the filling still show (see photo).

Peanut Butter Cups

🍬 **HOLIDAY** *Halloween*

🍬 **TYPE** *Molded candy*   🍬 **HABITAT** *United States*

🍬 **DESCRIPTION** *These are even better than store-bought, with milk chocolate on the outside and a creamy, salty peanut butter filling inside.*

🍬 **FIELD NOTES** *There are two ways to go about making these: either with purchased plastic molds in the classic patty shape, or with fluted muffin papers and a standard-size muffin tin. I give directions for both. The use of reduced-fat peanut butter is a trick I learned from an avid candy-making friend. The texture just seems to better approximate the popular commercial version. Feel free to use dark or white chocolate instead of milk chocolate.*

🍬 **LIFESPAN** *1 month refrigerated in airtight container in single layers separated by waxed or parchment paper*

Yield: *24 peanut butter cups*

Tools: *2 standard-size muffin tins with 12 wells each and 24 standard-size fluted muffin papers, or 24 flexible plastic patty-shaped molds, about 2¹/₄ inches wide (across the top) by ¹/₂ inch deep*

⌬ INGREDIENTS

14 ounces couverture milk chocolate (see page 10), finely chopped
1 cup reduced-fat peanut butter (hydrogenated style, not natural)

¹/₂ cup confectioners' sugar
¹/₈ teaspoon salt

⌬ DIRECTIONS

1. If you are using muffin tins and papers, cut each muffin paper halfway down from the top so that you are left with the bottom intact. The cup should be about ¹/₂ inch deep. The straighter you make your cut, the better looking your candies will be. If you are using plastic molds, wipe them with a clean soft dishcloth to remove any dust.

2. Melt the chocolate in a double boiler or in a medium-size bowl in the microwave. If using muffin papers, scoop a teaspoon of chocolate into the bottom of each cup and use the teaspoon to bring the chocolate up the sides, coating the inside of each cup as thoroughly and evenly as possible. Place each muffin paper in a muffin tin well to hold its shape. Refrigerate until completely firm, about 30 minutes, or 15 minutes in the freezer.

3. If using molds, proceed the same way with the chocolate and chill as directed above.

4. Meanwhile, make the filling. In a medium bowl with an electric mixer on low speed, beat the peanut butter, confectioners' sugar, and salt until combined. Turn speed to medium-high and beat until very creamy, about 2 minutes.

5. Place a scant tablespoon of filling in each chocolate patty. Dampen your fingers with cold water and pat the filling into the cup, filling up space widthwise but leaving some headroom.

6. Rewarm chocolate if necessary (it should be fluid). Spoon a generous teaspoon of chocolate on top of each cup and quickly but gently spread over the filling to seal it completely, using a small offset spatula.

7. Refrigerate until completely set, about 1 hour, or freeze for about 30 minutes.

8. If you used the muffin papers, serve the candies as is. If you used the molds, spread a piece of aluminum foil on the counter, turn the mold upside down, and gently press the patties out individually. The cups should pop out. (You might have to give the mold a gentle twist.)

Candy Tidbits

There is an alternate technique that can give the tops of your cups a very smooth look. After you have spooned the melted chocolate on top of the filling, tilt the muffin tin or mold this way and that so that the chocolate flows over the filling and fills in the spaces. This way you might not have to swipe a spatula over them at all, which can sometimes leave marks.

Easy Marbled Candy Corn Bark

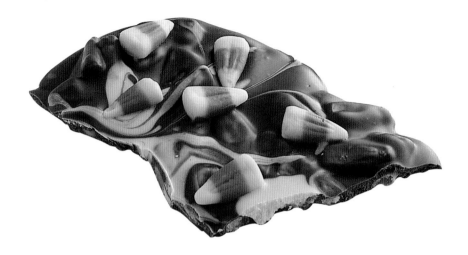

⋑●⋐ HOLIDAY *Halloween*

⋑●⋐ TYPE *Poured candy*   **⋑●⋐ HABITAT** *United States*

⋑●⋐ DESCRIPTION *This bark-style candy is super easy to make and comes together in a flash. It is also very sweet. Featuring milk and white chocolate and candy corn, this is best reserved for kids or adults with a major sweet tooth. It is perfect for school parties too.*

⋑●⋐ FIELD NOTES *The rest of the bark candies in this book use tempered chocolate, which yields a sophisticated texture, full of snap and crispness. However, it takes time to temper the chocolate. This recipe is meant to appeal to kids, in terms of preparing it as well as eating it. Here you simply melt the chocolates and proceed; just be sure to keep the bark refrigerated to retain its freshness.*

⋑●⋐ LIFESPAN *1 month refrigerated in airtight container in single layers separated by waxed or parchment paper*

Yield: *about 2¹/₄ pounds*

⊃●⊰ INGREDIENTS

1 pound couverture (see page 10) or regular milk chocolate, finely chopped

12 ounces couverture (see page 10) or regular white chocolate, finely chopped

1¹/₄ cups candy corn

⊃●⊰ DIRECTIONS

1. Line a jelly-roll pan with aluminum foil, smoothing out any wrinkles.

2. Melt milk and white chocolates separately in a double boiler or in medium-size bowls in the microwave. Fold half of the candy corn into the milk chocolate and spread this mixture onto the prepared pan in an even layer using an offset spatula. It doesn't have to be perfectly rectangular like the pan, as the candy will be broken up into random pieces.

3. While milk chocolate mixture is wet, dollop tablespoonfuls of white chocolate here and there over surface. Use the tip of a butter knife to swirl chocolates together. Do not overswirl or you will lose the definition of the milk and white chocolates.

4. While mixture is still wet, sprinkle remaining candy corn over the top and press in gently with fingers to help it adhere. Place bark in refrigerator until completely firm, about 30 minutes.

5. Peel off the aluminum foil. Break the bark into irregular pieces and enjoy!

Spider Webs

🕷 **HOLIDAY** *Halloween*

🕷 **TYPE** *Hand-formed candy*   🕷 **HABITAT** *United States*

🕷 **DESCRIPTION** *These should appeal to the very young, but then again, the combination of salty, crunchy pretzels and creamy, sweet white chocolate has grown-up appeal as well. You can use an extra-large semisweet chocolate chip for the "spider" or buy cute little spider candies from Wilton (see Resources).*

🕷 **FIELD NOTES** *These are very delicate and are best served at a Halloween party at home. They do not travel or store well. You will have plenty of pretzels left over for snacks.*

🕷 **LIFESPAN** *Best served soon after they are made (or if you have room for the pans in the refrigerator, they may sit overnight)*

Yield: *10 webs*

⊱●⊰ INGREDIENTS

One 15-ounce bag thin pretzel sticks
(about 2$\frac{1}{4}$ inches long)

5 ounces white chocolate, finely chopped

10 extra-large semisweet chocolate chips
or small candy spiders

⊱●⊰ DIRECTIONS

1. Line 2 jelly-roll pans with aluminum foil, smoothing out any wrinkles. Coat foil with nonstick cooking spray.

2. Five spider webs will fit on each pan. Using 12 pretzels to make each web, assemble the pretzels in a spoke pattern, spacing the individual webs apart from one another on the pan. The pretzels should touch in the center of each web and be evenly spaced apart from one another within each web (like spokes on a wheel).

3. Melt the chocolate in a double boiler or in a small bowl in the microwave and place in a zipper-lock plastic bag (you will have to use a few bags). Cut a small opening in the bottom corner of the bag and pipe a generous dollop of chocolate in the center of each web. Pipe concentric circles around and around the pretzel "spokes," going almost to the end of the pretzels (see photo). Place "spider" slightly off-center while chocolate is still wet. Chill webs until chocolate is firm.

Candy Tidbits

You can make as many as you like; you just need more pans and lots of refrigerator space. Per spider web, the formula is $\frac{1}{2}$ ounce chocolate, 12 pretzel sticks, and 1 "spider."

Give 'Em the Eyeball Candies

🍬 **HOLIDAY** *Halloween*

🍬 **TYPE** *Hand-formed candy*   🍬 **HABITAT** *United States*

🍬 **DESCRIPTION** *When we say, "Give 'em the eyeball," or, more usually, "Don't give me the eyeball," it usually carries a negative connotation, one of giving someone a look of disapproval or disdain. Here it is perfectly acceptable to hand someone one of these candies, which is a peanut butter "eyeball" decorated with "bloody" red-tinted chocolate. My son Freeman came up with this idea.*

🍬 **FIELD NOTES** *Okay, these are not health food, nor do they feature fine expensive chocolate or other ingredients. They are best made with the white chocolate coating, as suggested, as it is easier to work with than white chocolate. And this candy is all about the look, although if you like peanut butter, you will thoroughly enjoy the taste too.*

🍬 **LIFESPAN** *1 week refrigerated in airtight container in single layer*

Yield: *20 eyeballs*

❧●❧ INGREDIENTS

½ cup hydrogenated peanut butter (such as Skippy)

3 tablespoons unsalted butter, cut into pieces

1¼ cups confectioners' sugar, sifted

6 ounces white chocolate coating (see page 10), finely chopped

20 round brown candy-coated chocolate candies (such as M&M's)

Red paste or gel food coloring

❧●❧ DIRECTIONS

1. Line 2 jelly-roll pans with aluminum foil, smoothing out any wrinkles. Coat foil with nonstick cooking spray.

2. In a large bowl with an electric mixer on medium speed, beat peanut butter, butter, and confectioners' sugar until creamy and smooth.

3. Roll into 1-inch balls between your palms and place on prepared pan; freeze for 30 minutes.

4. Melt chocolate coating in a double boiler or microwave and stir until smooth. Dip balls into chocolate one at a time until completely coated, using your fingers, 2 forks, or chocolate dip-ping tools. Remove balls from chocolate, let excess chocolate drip back into pot, and place balls back on pan. Press 1 brown candy into each ball; these are the eyeball's irises. Chill until firm, about 30 minutes.

5. Tint the remaining chocolate coating with red coloring. Scrape into a zipper-lock plastic bag. Snip a small opening in a bottom corner of the bag and pipe bloody squiggles onto each eyeball. Chill until red chocolate is firm, about 15 minutes.

Candy Tidbits

You could use any color of the candy-coated chocolate candy for the "iris." I just think the dark brown adds to the sinister look of the bloody eyeballs. (I have brown eyes, so I can say that!)

Sugar Skulls

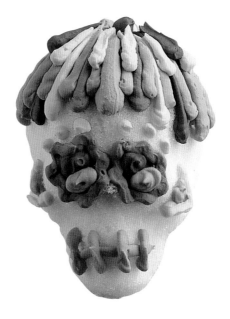

🍬 **HOLIDAY** *Day of the Dead*

🍬 **TYPE** *Molded candy* 🍬 **HABITAT** *Mexico*

🍬 **DESCRIPTION** *These molded skulls are made from sugar and decorated with multicolored icing. While they are theoretically edible, they are used for decorative purposes.*

🍬 **FIELD NOTES** *Skull imagery may seem morbid, but in Mexico, the Day of the Dead is a holiday that celebrates the lives of those who have departed. It is a two-day holiday celebrated on All Saint's Day (November 1) and All Soul's Day (November 2). Colorful and gay skulls adorn altars and graves as a way of welcoming spirits back for a visit. The name of a specific loved one often adorns the skull. Children are involved in the making of the skulls to help them remember those who are deceased. You will need a skull mold and meringue powder as well as many bright food colors (see Resources for supplies). The sugar skulls require two overnight drying periods, so plan accordingly, and do not attempt this recipe on a very humid day.*

🍬 **LIFESPAN** *Years at room temperature in airtight container*

Yield: *10 skulls*

Tools: *1 medium-size skull mold (about 3 inches) • Ten 6-inch cardboard rounds*

INGREDIENTS

5¹/₄ cups granulated sugar
2 tablespoons meringue powder
I to 2 tablespoons water

Icing:
6¹/₂ to 7¹/₂ cups confectioners' sugar, sifted
¹/₂ cup meringue powder
²/₃ cup water
Paste food coloring

DIRECTIONS

1. Wipe the skull mold with a clean soft dishcloth to remove any dust.

2. Whisk sugar and meringue powder together in a large bowl. Sprinkle 1 tablespoon water over sugar and whisk the mixture, then mix with your hands until sugar is moist enough that it holds together when you squeeze a clump. Add more water if necessary. It will probably need just shy of 2 tablespoons water.

3. Pack sugar mixture into mold, mounding it over the top. Press it firmly down into mold, using an offset spatula to evenly wipe away excess. Sugar should come right up to the open edge of the mold and fill in any crevices that form the shape of the skull's face. Lift the mold high enough so that you can see the side with the skull imprint. Check to see that all nooks and crannies are completely filled with sugar.

4. Place a piece of cardboard on top of the open side and carefully invert the mold. Place cardboard on work surface and very carefully remove the mold.

You should have a well-formed and detailed sugar skull on the piece of cardboard. If the skull is not to your liking (and this is simply a matter of whether you like the way it looks or not), simply reuse the sugar and try again. If the sugar is too dry, it will crumble. If it is too wet, the skull will have soft features and flow down toward the cardboard. Add more sugar or water, if necessary, until you have the right texture and you have made 10 skulls.

5. Allow skulls, still on cardboards, to dry overnight.

6. To make icing, beat 6¹/₂ cups confectioners' sugar, meringue powder, and water with an electric mixer on medium speed until smooth and fluffy. Add more sugar if necessary to attain a stiff texture. Divide it into several bowls and tint as desired with various food colorings. Place each color in a zipper-lock plastic bag. Snip a small opening in a bottom corner of the bag and decorate skull as desired. Allow icing to dry overnight.

Harvest Fruit 'n' Nut Bark

⚊●⚊ **HOLIDAY** *Thanksgiving*

⚊●⚊ **TYPE** *Poured candy*   ⚊●⚊ **HABITAT** *United States*

⚊●⚊ **DESCRIPTION** *Bark-style candies are easy to make, as they simply combine chocolate with various add-ins such as nuts and, in this case, dried fruit. The combination of fruit and nuts makes this bark reminiscent of harvest time, hence its Thanksgiving association.*

⚊●⚊ **FIELD NOTES** *As with any chocolate bark recipe, you may temper the chocolate for a crisp texture, or you may simply melt the chocolate and proceed. If you eliminate tempering, make sure to keep the bark refrigerated at all times or the chocolate might "bloom" and streak. This is simply the cocoa butter coming to the surface, which will not harm the taste, but it does affect both the appearance and texture of the bark.*

⚊●⚊ **LIFESPAN** *1 month refrigerated in airtight container in single layers separated by waxed or parchment paper*

Yield: *about 2 pounds*

◖●◗ INGREDIENTS

¹/₂ cup dried cranberries
¹/₂ cup chopped apricots (¹/₄-inch size)
¹/₂ cup whole peeled, toasted hazelnuts
  (see page 16)

¹/₂ cup chopped, toasted Brazil nuts
  (¹/₂-inch size, see page 16)
1 pound couverture bittersweet or
  semisweet chocolate (see page 10) or
  regular chocolate, finely chopped

◖●◗ DIRECTIONS

1. Line a jelly-roll pan with aluminum foil, shiny side up, smoothing out any wrinkles, or line the pan with a piece of acetate.

2. In a medium-size bowl, toss fruit and nuts together and divide in half.

3. Temper bittersweet chocolate according to the directions on page 14, or melt over low heat in a double boiler or in a large bowl in a microwave. Gently stir in half of the fruit and nut mixture, then spread in an even layer over the aluminum foil using an offset spatula. It doesn't have to be perfectly rectangular like the pan, as the candy will be broken up into random pieces.

4. While chocolate mixture is wet, sprinkle remaining fruit and nut mixture over top and press in gently with your fingers to help it adhere. Place bark in refrigerator until completely firm, about 30 minutes.

5. Peel off the aluminum foil. Break the bark into irregular pieces and enjoy!

Candy Tidbits

You can, of course, substitute an equal amount of milk or white chocolate for the bittersweet, and vary the fruits and nuts. Some others to consider: macadamias, pistachios, walnuts, dried cherries, golden raisins. The sky's the limit!

Spiced Pumpkin Pecan Fudge

▷●◁ **HOLIDAY** *Thanksgiving, Halloween*

▷●◁ **TYPE** *Bar candy*   ▷●◁ **HABITAT** *United States*

▷●◁ **DESCRIPTION** *When you hear the word* fudge *you probably think* chocolate. *This recipe does have chocolate in it. It's just that it is melted white chocolate that adds body and a background flavor to an otherwise pumpkin-flavored confection. The ingredients call for canned pumpkin and spices such as ginger, cinnamon, nutmeg, and cloves, making the recipe reminiscent of pumpkin pie. A few pecans add crunch. As with most fudge, this is for those with sweet teeth (or is that sweet tooths?).*

▷●◁ **FIELD NOTES** *This fudge utilizes marshmallow creme, such as Fluff, as an ingredient. It has a remarkable ability to make fudge that is ultra-creamy. This is an extremely user-friendly fudge recipe. While I do suggest a thermometer here, the marshmallow will all but guarantee great results.*

▷●◁ **LIFESPAN** *2 weeks refrigerated in airtight container in single layers separated by waxed or parchment paper*

Yield: *48 fudge squares*

⊜⊛⊰ INGREDIENTS

12 tablespoons (1½ sticks) unsalted
  butter, cut into pieces
3 cups granulated sugar
²/₃ cup evaporated milk
²/₃ cup canned pumpkin puree
½ teaspoon ground cinnamon
½ teaspoon ground ginger

⅛ teaspoon ground nutmeg
Pinch ground cloves
12 ounces white chocolate, finely chopped
One 7½-ounce jar (about 1½ cups)
  marshmallow creme, such as Fluff
¾ cup toasted pecan halves (see page 16),
  chopped

⊜⊛⊰ DIRECTIONS

1. Coat a 9 x 13-inch baking pan with nonstick cooking spray.

2. Stir together butter, sugar, evaporated milk, pumpkin, and spices in a large saucepan. Bring to a boil over medium heat, stirring constantly until it reaches 235°F (soft-ball stage).

3. Remove from heat and stir in chopped chocolate until chocolate melts. Stir in marshmallow creme until mixture is smooth. Stir in nuts and scrape into prepared pan,

smoothing the top with an offset spatula. Cool to room temperature.

4. Refrigerate overnight or until completely firm. Cut into 48 squares (6 x 8).

Candy Tidbits

If you can find the specific size jar of Fluff, buy it. Fluff is very hard to measure because it is so sticky; it is much easier if you can just scrape out the whole jar. Also, to make these fancier you can place a whole pecan half on each piece. Do this by eye while mixture is still soft so the nut adheres.

Chocolate Leaves

⊱●⊰ HOLIDAY *Thanksgiving*

⊱●⊰ TYPE *Hand-formed candy*   **⊱●⊰ HABITAT** *United States*

⊱●⊰ DESCRIPTION *These are pure chocolate molded on real leaves so that the veins and texture of the leaves are transferred to the candy. The milk chocolate gives a pale brown look; the butterscotch chips resemble fall foliage. You can marbleize a variety of flavors and colors, and all may be embellished with powder colors to create a realistic autumnal look. They look (and taste) great as an adornment to Thanksgiving desserts.*

⊱●⊰ FIELD NOTES *Some good leaves to try are lemon and grape leaves, which can be purchased from a florist. Small ones are easier to work with. You also need a soft brush; you can buy tiny, 1/2-inch wide pastry brushes that are perfect. You don't have to temper the chocolates because the leaves, which are very delicate, will be kept refrigerated. The powdered colors can be ordered from Beryl's (see Resources).*

⊱●⊰ LIFESPAN *1 week refrigerated in airtight container in a single layer*

Yield: *25 to 30 leaves, depending on size and candy breakage*

Tools: *30 small lemon or grape leaves, washed and dried • Three ¹/₂-inch wide pastry brushes or small artist's paint brushes*

✒●✑ INGREDIENTS

6 ounces butterscotch chips
6 ounces couverture milk chocolate
(see page 10), finely chopped

6 ounces couverture white chocolate
(see page 10), finely chopped
Powder food colorings such as rust, deep
yellow, orange, green, brown

✒●✑ DIRECTIONS

1. Line 2 jelly-roll pans with aluminum foil, shiny side up, smoothing out any wrinkles, or line pans with pieces of acetate.

2. Melt butterscotch chips and chocolates individually in double boilers or the microwave.

3. Now you have some options. You can make each leaf one flavor, or you can marbleize two of them. Use a different brush for each flavor. For one flavor, hold a leaf by the stem and use a brush to paint the underside of the leaf with one flavor, taking care not to go over onto the top of the leaf. Aim for a thin, even layer. Place the leaves spaced apart on prepared pan and chill until firm, about 30 minutes.

4. For marbleizing, paint portions of the underside of a leaf with melted butterscotch; chill until firm, about 20 minutes. Now paint the entire underside, including the part you've already painted, with either the milk or white chocolate. Chill until firm, about 30 minutes.

5. If you make these ahead, do not peel them until needed; the real leaf will protect the chocolate leaf. To peel, gently hold the leaf's sides, grasp the stem, and begin to peel it off of the chocolate. If you meet with any resistance, try peeling another section of leaf first.

Candy Tidbits

For a ritzy look, you can embellish any of the chocolate colors with gold powder (also from Beryl's). Or you could try flavoring the chocolate with mint oil and painting tiny mint leaves. Leaves with a lot of ruffles and ridges are more difficult and some mint is curly, so look for mint with a smooth leaf surface.

Coconut Cashew Burfi

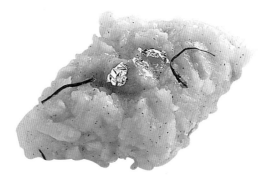

▷●◁ **HOLIDAY** *Diwali (Indian Festival of Lights)*

▷●◁ **TYPE** *Bar candy*   ▷●◁ **HABITAT** *India*

▷●◁ **DESCRIPTION** *Burfi is essentially a very sweet milk fudge. My recipe features coconut and cashews, which are added to fancier versions in India. Pistachios or almonds may be used as well, and I have even heard of layered versions that have different nuts in each layer.*

▷●◁ **FIELD NOTES** *Diwali is similar to Christmas in that electric lights and decorations festoon city streets, presents are bought and given, and homes are decorated to receive guests. Burfi, also spelled "barfi," is an example of a traditional confection that can be made at home, but that is often bought ready-made. You need clarified butter, or ghee, for this recipe. It is hard to clarify a tiny amount, so I suggest starting with ¹/₂ cup. Melt it gently over medium heat in a small saucepan, carefully skimming off any foam that rises to the top. Pour the clarified butter into another container, leaving behind the milk solids. The ghee is now ready to use.*

▷●◁ **LIFESPAN** *2 weeks refrigerated in airtight container in single layers separated by waxed or parchment paper*

Yield: *about 20 diamonds*

Tools: *Tweezers*

►●◄ INGREDIENTS

2 tablespoons ghee (clarified butter)
1 cup unsweetened grated coconut
3/4 cup granulated sugar
1 cup milk

1/2 teaspoon ground cardamom
Pinch of saffron
1/3 cup roasted cashews, coarsely chopped
Silver leaf

►●◄ DIRECTIONS

1. Coat an 8-inch square baking pan with nonstick cooking spray.

2. Heat ghee in a medium-size saucepan over medium heat and add coconut. Stir until coconut absorbs all of the ghee and begins to dry out. It will make a crackling sound when the ghee is completely absorbed.

3. Stir in sugar, milk, cardamom, and saffron and bring to a boil. Simmer gently until the mixture is very thick, stirring occasionally. It will darken a bit and turn golden, about 12 minutes. You should be able to see the bottom of the pan for a moment when you draw a spoon through the mixture.

4. Remove from heat, stir in cashews, and scrape into the prepared pan, smoothing the top with an offset spatula. Cool to room temperature, then refrigerate until firm, about 1 hour.

5. Cut into diamonds. Use tweezers to pick up little bits of silver leaf and place in center of diamonds (it will adhere).

Candy Tidbits

I have also added a bit of silver leaf, which is a traditional yet extra-special embellishment for Indian confections and foods. Look in art supply stores for pure silver, free of aluminum or other metals.

Sugar Candies (Borstplaat)

⋙●⋘ **HOLIDAY** *St. Nicholas's Day*

⋙●⋘ **TYPE** *Drop candy*   ⋙●⋘ **HABITAT** *Holland*

⋙●⋘ **DESCRIPTION** *These are very easy to make, very sugary candies, which you might variously find made with fruit flavors, coffee, or chocolate. This version is fruity (limey, actually).*

⋙●⋘ **FIELD NOTES** *This candy will be a bit unusual to American palates, as it is basically pure sugar with an interesting sandy texture. Borstplaat are simply sugar patties with a little bit of flavoring added, and you will find them in shops in Holland for St. Nicholas's Day, which falls on December 6. You must stop stirring the sugar mixture as soon as the spoon feels scratchy against the bottom of the pan or else the candy will set up in the pan. You must also drop the candies onto the prepared pan quickly! Two hands are helpful here.*

⋙●⋘ **LIFESPAN** *2 weeks at room temperature in airtight container in single layers separated by waxed or parchment paper*

Yield: *20 tiny patties*

✎●✑ INGREDIENTS

1³/₄ cups water
¹/₂ cup granulated sugar

Lime oil
Green liquid food coloring

✎●✑ DIRECTIONS

1. Line a jelly-roll pan with aluminum foil, smoothing out any wrinkles. Coat foil with nonstick cooking spray.

2. Stir water and sugar together in a medium-size saucepan. Bring to a boil over medium-high heat and cook to 235°F (soft-ball stage), about 10 minutes. Remove from heat and gently stir in lime oil and coloring.

3. Continue to stir gently; mixture will begin to turn cloudy and white-ish. Keep stirring until it is opaque and you feel some gritty scratchiness beneath the spoon in the pot. These are sugar crystals

forming. Use a teaspoon to drop one 1-inch round patty on the prepared pan. Mixture is ready if it holds its shape and sets up quickly. Very quickly spoon out the patties. Allow candies to firm up at room temperature.

Candy Tidbits

An easy way to vary the flavor is to try orange oil with a drop of red food coloring and a drop of yellow food coloring, or lemon oil with a drop of yellow food coloring. Just don't try to divide one batch into different flavors; the candy sets up too quickly for that.

Candy Dreidels

✈●✦ **HOLIDAY** *Hanukkah*

✈●✦ **TYPE** *Hand-formed candy*   ✈●✦ **HABITAT** *United States*

✈●✦ **DESCRIPTION** *This is so easy! Chocolate kisses and marshmallows combine to make edible dreidels, or spinning tops. There is no cooking involved, which makes them perfect for even the youngest children to make. (These tops do not work well for spinning, but of course they are good to eat.)*

✈●✦ **FIELD NOTES** *At Hanukkah children play a game in which dreidels (tops) are spun and the players can win gelt, or money, which is sometimes real coins but more often foil-covered chocolate coins. The sides of the dreidel have lettering that "spells" out "[a] great miracle happened there" (referring to Israel). For complete directions on how to play, go to www.holidays.net/chanukah/dreidel. These candy dreidels can be made with very small children as a way of encouraging them in the kitchen while teaching them about the holiday. I first saw these at a school party and later learned that Joan Nathan has a version in her* Children's Jewish Holiday Kitchen *(Schocken, 2000).*

✈●✦ **LIFESPAN** *1 week at room temperature in airtight container*

Yield: *20 dreidels*

⋟●⋞ INGREDIENTS

20 foil-wrapped chocolate kisses
20 regular-size marshmallows
20 toothpicks with blue cellophane frills

Blue and yellow felt-tip food-safe markers, such as Wilton Food Writer or Betty Crocker Easy Writer

⋟●⋞ DIRECTIONS

1. Remove any paper strips protruding from the foil-wrapped kiss; just snip them off with scissors. Place a marshmallow on top of the flat end of a kiss. Insert a toothpick all the way down through the marshmallow until it skewers the chocolate kiss, holding the two together. You should now have a top-shaped dreidel!

2. Using photo for guidance, use yellow marker to place yellow dots evenly spaced around top and bottom of marshmallow. Use blue marker to place the four Hebrew letters evenly spaced around center portion of marshmallow (see www.holidays.net/chanukah/dreidel for the letters).

Candy Tidbits

There are a variety of foil-wrapped chocolate kisses on the market, so feel free to experiment. Some are milk chocolate, some dark, some striped with different flavors. And since they come wrapped with different-colored foils, you can get different looks. The Betty Crocker markers can be found in supermarkets nationwide. The Wilton brand markers can be purchased direct from Wilton (see Resources).

Peppermint Patties

≫●≪ HOLIDAY *Winter solstice*

≫●≪ TYPE *Hand-formed candy*   **≫●≪ HABITAT** *United States*

≫●≪ DESCRIPTION *These feature a snow-white, creamy, and very minty filling surrounded by a bittersweet or semisweet chocolate coating. The chocolate-shortening combo makes these very easy to dip (do not substitute anything else for the shortening). Alternatively, you may temper the chocolate and eliminate the shortening, but it makes the recipe longer and more involved.*

≫●≪ FIELD NOTES *Make sure to use Frontier brand peppermint flavoring, as it is the one I used to test this recipe and the quality and strength of peppermint flavor varies from brand to brand. Frontier will give you a true peppermint taste that an extract just cannot approximate. I associate name-brand candies with Halloween, as they are usually the ones given out for trick-or-treating, but these would certainly be welcomed at any time of year, and the minty white filling reminds me of winter.*

≫●≪ LIFESPAN *1 month refrigerated in airtight container in single layers separated by waxed or parchment paper*

Yield: *40 patties*

➽●⬳ INGREDIENTS

2 cups confectioners' sugar
1½ tablespoons unsalted butter, softened
1½ teaspoons Frontier peppermint
  flavoring
¼ teaspoon vanilla extract

2 tablespoons evaporated milk
9 ounces bittersweet or semisweet
  chocolate, finely chopped
1 tablespoon shortening

➽●⬳ DIRECTIONS

1. Line a jelly-roll pan with aluminum foil, shiny side up, smoothing out any wrinkles. Coat foil with nonstick cooking spray.

2. In a large bowl with an electric mixer on low speed, beat the confectioners' sugar, butter, peppermint flavoring, vanilla extract, and evaporated milk until combined. Turn speed to medium-high and beat until very creamy, about 3 minutes. Chill for 30 minutes or until firm enough to roll.

3. Roll filling into 1-inch balls and place on prepared pan. Flatten using your palms or fingers until patties are about 1½ inches wide and ⅓ inch high. Chill again until firm, about 30 minutes.

4. Melt chocolate and shortening (or temper chocolate without shortening according to the directions on page 14) in a double boiler or in a medium-size bowl in the microwave, stirring until smooth. Dip patties into chocolate one at a time until completely coated, using your fingers, 2 forks, or chocolate dipping tools. Remove patties from chocolate, let excess chocolate drip back into pot, and place patties back on foil. Chill until firm, about 30 minutes.

Candy Tidbits

Any candy or baked good made with peppermint will impart that flavor and aroma to other items stored alongside, so make sure to store these separately from other foods. I go so far as to wrap them individually when I present them on a tray or pack them in a box so that they don't lend their aroma to the other candies.

Candy Canes

⟩●⟨ **HOLIDAY** *Christmas*

⟩●⟨ **TYPE** *Pulled candy*   ⟩●⟨ **HABITAT** *United States and Germany*

⟩●⟨ **DESCRIPTION** *This is a pulled candy, which means it is a sugar mixture that is boiled, cooled, flavored, pulled, and shaped. The classic flavor, as is described here, is peppermint, but you could certainly use other flavors and accompanying colors.*

⟩●⟨ **FIELD NOTES** *Some historians date candy canes back to Germany in the 1670s. Legend has it that an ingenious church choirmaster in seventeenth-century Germany invented the candy, made to resemble a shepherd's crook, as a distraction for some noisy children in the church. The traditional red color is supposed to signify Christ's blood, while the mint flavor is reminiscent of hyssop, an herb used in biblical times. Who knows who first hung them on Christmas trees, but their shape obviously lends them to this now-common practice. They are a fun family project for school vacation. Adults should supervise the hot sugar syrup, but the pulling process benefits from extra hands.*

⟩●⟨ **LIFESPAN** *1 month at room temperature in single layers separated by waxed or parchment paper*

Yield: *about 15 canes*

Tools: *4 jelly-roll pans or 9 x 13-inch baking pans • 2 metal bench scrapers • 2 pairs heavy-duty rubber gloves • Scissors • Cellophane*

ᗦ●᙭ INGREDIENTS

3 cups granulated sugar

1 cup light corn syrup

1/4 cup water

1/4 teaspoon peppermint oil

Generous 1/4 teaspoon red paste or gel food coloring

Candy Tidbits

Don't overwork the two colors together or they will blend and you won't have stripes anymore. Some folks like to roll the candy into long cylinders on an oiled surface to get the right shape before cutting. I would approach this recipe as a grand experiment; the candy might end up looking different than store-bought, but it is so much more special.

ᗦ●᙭ DIRECTIONS

1. Preheat oven to 200°F. Generously oil jelly-roll pans, the surface of the bench scrapers, the fingers and palms of the gloves, and the scissors with canola oil.

2. Stir sugar, corn syrup, and water together in a medium-size saucepan. Bring to a boil over medium-high heat to 285°F (soft-crack stage), about 12 minutes.

3. Remove from heat and add peppermint oil, swirling pot to incorporate. Immediately pour half the mixture onto one prepared pan and place in oven. Add red food coloring to remaining mixture, swirl pan to begin to incorporate color, and quickly pour onto second pan. The color will not be fully distributed.

4. Let pan with red half sit at room temperature for a few minutes. The sugar will begin to firm up; gently bring the edges of the puddle onto itself, repeatedly scraping edges toward the middle using a bench scraper. The color will begin to blend. Keep doing this until the mixture is cool enough to handle—but it must remain warm or you will not be able to pull it.

5. Put on the gloves, pick up red half, and begin to stretch and pull, stretch and pull. This is where it is helpful to have another person, dividing the mixture so that each can take half. As you work, the candy will cool and become somewhat satiny and opaque. Keep manipulating it until it is solid red, satiny, and just warm. Shape it into long ropes about 2 inches wide and place back on greased pan. Place in oven.

6. Remove uncolored half from oven. Repeat the stretching and pulling process. The mixture should turn white; place pan back in oven.

7. Use an oiled bench scraper to cut off a piece of white and a piece of red. Form them into logs and place each white log right next to a red log on the third oiled pan, which is now your work surface. Pick up a bicolored log and start to pull and stretch and slightly twist at the same time, going for the classic look and size of candy canes. Use the scissors to cut off lengths of about 8 inches, and immediately bend the top of each one into a hook shape. Place the canes on the fourth pan to cool at room temperature.

8. Repeat with remaining candy. If at any point the candy gets too hard, simply return it to the oven until it softens. Wrap the canes individually in cellophane, if desired.

Ribbon Candy

⊸●⊷ **HOLIDAY** *Christmas*

⊸●⊷ **TYPE** *Pulled candy*   ⊸●⊷ **HABITAT** *United States*

⊸●⊷ **DESCRIPTION** *Like the candy canes on page 126, this is a pulled candy. You could flavor it any which way, but I chose peppermint with a red, white, and green color palette.*

⊸●⊷ **FIELD NOTES** *I don't want to be accused of leading you astray, so let me state up front that this is the most difficult recipe in the book—but it is also the most rewarding and fun! The main problem people have is that the candy gets hard too quickly. Just place it back in the oven and let it soften. Here's a technique to get the candy as thin as possible: One of you picks up a tricolored log and starts to press it out thinly, an inch at a time, using your thumbs and index fingers, pressing it away from you. The other person grabs that thinned part and begins to stretch and pull the candy away from you, immediately forming the accordion ribbon shape as they go. Working together on the same piece of candy makes the process go more quickly.*

⊸●⊷ **LIFESPAN** *1 month at room temperature in single layers separated by waxed or parchment paper*

Yield: *about 25 ribbons of candy*

Tools: *5 jelly-roll pans or 9 x 13-inch baking pans • 3 metal bench scrapers • 2 pairs heavy-duty rubber gloves • Scissors*

⟩●⟨ INGREDIENTS

3 cups granulated sugar
1 cup light corn syrup
¹/₄ cup water
¹/₄ teaspoon peppermint oil

Generous ¹/₄ teaspoon green paste food coloring
Generous ¹/₄ teaspoon red paste food coloring

⟩●⟨ DIRECTIONS

1. Preheat oven to 200°F. Generously oil pans, the surface of the bench scrapers, the fingers and palms of the gloves, and the scissors with canola oil.

2. Stir together sugar, corn syrup, and water in a medium-size saucepan. Bring to a boil over medium-high heat to 285°F (soft-crack stage), about 12 minutes.

3. Remove from heat and add peppermint oil, swirling pot to incorporate. Immediately pour about one-third of the mixture onto 1 pan and place in oven. Pour another third onto another pan and place green food coloring on top; place in oven. Pour remaining mixture onto third pan and place red food coloring on top.

4. Let pan with red mixture sit at room temperature for a few minutes. The sugar will begin to firm up; gently bring the edges of the puddle onto itself, repeatedly scraping the edges toward the middle using a bench scraper. The color will begin to blend in. Keep doing this until the mixture is cool enough to handle but remains warm, or you will not be able to pull it.

5. Put on the gloves, pick up the red mass, and begin to stretch and pull; it is helpful to have another person, dividing the mixture in half. As you stretch and pull, the candy will cool and become somewhat satiny in appearance. Keep manipulating it until it is solid red, satiny, and just warm. Shape the two halves into long ropes about 2 inches wide and place back on greased pan. Place in oven.

6. Remove pan with green mixture from oven. Repeat the dividing, stretching, and pulling process; place back in oven. Remove the pan with the uncolored part and repeat process; place back in oven.

7. Use an oiled bench scraper to cut off a piece of white, a piece of red, and a piece of green. Form them into a big log on the fourth oiled pan, placing white strip in the middle of the red and green. Pick up log and start to pull and stretch gently, but deliberately. You want to end up with a ribbon of tricolored candy about 1-inch wide and as thin as can be. Working with lengths no greater than 18 inches will be easiest. (The scissors can help you cut pieces). Pull and stretch until you have a thin ribbon, then immediately accordion-fold the candy to form a ribbon (see photo) and place it on its side to cool at room temperature on the last pan.

8. Repeat with remaining candy. If at any point the candy gets too hard, simply return it to the oven until it softens.

Double Chocolate Peppermint Bark

●◄ **HOLIDAY** *Christmas*

●◄ **TYPE** *Poured candy*   ●◄ **HABITAT** *United States*

●◄ **DESCRIPTION** *This recipe features a layer of bittersweet chocolate topped with creamy white chocolate and crowned with a scattering of chopped red and white peppermint candy canes. The result is a crunchy, minty confection that is great for gift giving.*

●◄ **FIELD NOTES** *Perhaps you have seen expensive versions of this confection in upscale catalogs. It is a perfect example of something that can be purchased for a hefty price, but duplicated at home for a fraction of the cost. Also, with the homemade version you can use the highest-quality ingredients, resulting in an even better product. My friend Naomi Waynee sent me a similar recipe—great minds think alike. Actually, hers is much easier; she simply melts one type of chocolate, stirs in the crushed candy, and spreads it out to harden. Try that if you are short on time.*

●◄ **LIFESPAN** *1 month refrigerated in airtight container in single layers separated by waxed or parchment paper*

Yield: *about 2 pounds*

INGREDIENTS

Twelve 6- to 7-inch-long red and white peppermint candy canes

1 pound couverture bittersweet or semisweet chocolate (see page 10), finely chopped

1 pound couverture white chocolate (see page 10), finely chopped

DIRECTIONS

1. Line a jelly-roll pan with aluminum foil, shiny side up, smoothing out any wrinkles, or line the pan with a piece of acetate.

2. Place candy canes in a heavy-duty zipper-lock plastic bag, press out air, and seal bag. Crush candy canes with a rolling pin, alternately rolling and whacking candy until it is fairly uniformly crushed; aim for $1/4$-inch pieces. If there is a lot of powdery residue, place candy in a strainer and shake out and discard powdery part (or save and stir into hot chocolate). You may also chop candy in a food processor fitted with a metal blade, pulsing on and off. It will make a racket, however.

3. Temper bittersweet chocolate according to the directions on page 14 and spread in a thin, even layer (about $1/8$ inch) all over the aluminum foil using an offset spatula. It doesn't have to be perfectly rectangular like the pan, as the candy will be broken up into random pieces. Place in refrigerator to firm while you temper white chocolate.

4. Spread tempered white chocolate in a thin, even layer over bittersweet chocolate. Immediately sprinkle chopped candy over white chocolate while it is still wet. Place bark in refrigerator until completely firm, about 20 minutes.

5. Peel off the aluminum foil. Break the bark into irregular pieces and enjoy!

Candy Tidbits

This candy looks great packaged in clear cellophane bags tied with red, green, gold, or silver ribbons—perfect for a hostess gift during the holidays. Or go all out and offer a whole tin! Also, if you can find red, green, and white candy canes, the bark will look even more colorful.

Chocolate Walnut Rum Balls

HOLIDAY *Christmas*

TYPE *Hand-formed candy*   **HABITAT** *United States*

DESCRIPTION *No-bake confections such as these always seem to find their way into Christmas recipe collections since they are easy to prepare and make a great holiday gift. These are a combination of crushed cookie crumbs, ground nuts, sugar, chocolate, and rum. They are best if aged at least overnight, and are even better after a few days. Some say they hit their peak after a month, so plan accordingly.*

FIELD NOTES *There are many versions of rum- or bourbon-flavored balls featuring cookie crumbs, some dating back to the 1930s. Older versions often use cocoa instead of chocolate, probably because it was a more typical pantry item. The addition of corn syrup is newfangled as well and gives the balls a nice chewy texture.*

LIFESPAN *$1^{1}/_{2}$ months at room temperature in airtight container in single layers separated by waxed or parchment paper*

Yield: *50 balls*

❧●❧ INGREDIENTS

2 1/2 cups vanilla wafer crumbs (such as
Nabisco Nilla Wafers)
1/2 cup confectioners' sugar, sifted
1 cup toasted walnut halves (see page 16),
finely ground

6 ounces semisweet or bittersweet
chocolate, finely chopped
1/2 cup gold rum
3 tablespoons light corn syrup
Granulated sugar
50 small fluted paper cups (optional)

❧●❧ DIRECTIONS

1. Stir together cookie crumbs, confectioners' sugar, and nuts in a large bowl.

2. Melt chocolate in a double boiler or in
a medium-size bowl in the microwave.
Stir in rum and corn syrup. Add chocolate mixture to cookie-crumb mixture
and stir well to combine. Let mixture sit for 30 minutes. Place
some granulated sugar in a
small bowl.

3. Roll mixture between your
palms into 1-inch balls, then
roll in sugar. Place balls in airtight container and allow the

flavors to develop by sitting at room
temperature at least overnight. You
may first place them in small fluted
paper cups, if desired.

Candy Tidbits

You can try pecans instead of
walnuts in these. You can also make
bourbon balls by substituting a good-
quality bourbon for the rum, or even try
Grand Marnier or Kahlúa for orange or
coffee versions. Chocolate cookie
crumbs turn these into a very
decadent over-the-top
chocolatey confection.

Sugarplums

⊱●⊰ **HOLIDAY** *Christmas*

⊱●⊰ **TYPE** *Hand-formed candy*   ⊱●⊰ **HABITAT** *United States and Portugal*

⊱●⊰ **DESCRIPTION** *These small candies are made from a mélange of dried fruit and nuts. They are great to make with kids, using orange juice instead of alcohol. There are several ways to finish them off, and I suggest that you choose at least two of the options. You may roll them in granulated or confectioners' sugar, but since these candies are actually sugar-free, despite their name, I suggest trying the other toppings. My favorites are ground pistachios for their lovely green color, and additional coconut for a snowball effect. This is a recipe from* A Baker's Field Guide to Christmas Cookies *(The Harvard Common Press, 2003), but this time I have streamlined the preparation. It really does work to grind all the ingredients together at once!*

⊱●⊰ **FIELD NOTES** *The original version may have come from Portugal, where fresh black figs and cooked green plums were used to make a similar candy.*

⊱●⊰ **LIFESPAN** *1 month refrigerated in airtight container*

Yield: *65 sugarplums*

⋙●⋘ INGREDIENTS

1 cup toasted pecan halves (see page 16)
1/2 cup pitted dates
1/2 cup dried Calimyrna figs
1/2 cup pitted dried plums (prunes)
1/2 cup dried cherries
1/2 cup golden raisins
1/2 cup unsweetened grated coconut
1/4 cup rum, orange liqueur, or orange juice

Toppings (optional):
Finely chopped almonds, hazelnuts, pecans,
  pistachios, or walnuts
Finely grated bittersweet chocolate
Unsweetened Dutch-processed cocoa
  powder
Unsweetened grated coconut
Granulated sugar
Confectioners' sugar

65 small fluted paper cups (optional)

⋙●⋘ DIRECTIONS

1. The key to this recipe is to end up with all the nuts and fruits the same small size. You may chop them by hand or use a food processor fitted with a metal blade. Place all nuts and fruits in bowl of processor and pulse on and off until the desired size is reached; the mixture should be evenly and finely ground.

2. Place fruit and nut mixture, coconut, and liquid of choice in a medium-size bowl. Mix together by hand until thoroughly combined; the mixture should hold together when compressed. If it is dry, add a little more liquid.

3. Roll mixture into 1-inch balls, compressing the mixture so it sticks together. Place toppings of choice in small bowls and roll sugarplums in them, one by one, to coat completely. I like to leave some in their natural state as well. Place in small fluted paper cups, if desired.

Candy Tidbits

To measure small amounts of ingredients such as prunes, simply press them firmly into a 1/2-cup measuring cup.

Christmas Divinity

🍬 **TYPE** *Drop candy*   🍬 **HABITAT** *United States*

🍬 **DESCRIPTION** *Divinity begins with a cooked sugar syrup poured over beaten egg whites. From there you can add any number of flavors, such as nuts, chocolate, or candied fruit. My version contains diced candied lemon peel and slivered almonds.*

🍬 **FIELD NOTES** *This is a popular holiday sweet in the southeastern United States. The technique of adding sugar syrup in two phases, each boiled to a different stage, is typical of this confection. The tricky part of this recipe is having the egg whites and the sugar syrup ready at relatively the same time. Read the recipe through carefully before beginning so that you are prepared with the steps needed as they come up.*

🍬 **RELATED SPECIES** *Try Pineapple Cherry Divinity by using candied cherries and pineapple instead of the lemon and almonds, or Chocolate Walnut Divinity by substituting chocolate chips and chopped walnuts. I have also seen minty pink variations using red food coloring and a few drops of peppermint or spearmint extract in lieu of the almond and vanilla.*

🍬 **LIFESPAN** *2 weeks at room temperature in single layers separated by waxed or parchment paper*

Yield: *40 candies*

ꜱ●꜕ INGREDIENTS

2¹/₂ cups sugar
¹/₂ cup light corn syrup
¹/₂ cup water
2 large egg whites
Pinch of salt

¹/₂ teaspoon almond extract
¹/₂ teaspoon vanilla extract
¹/₂ cup diced candied lemon peel
¹/₂ cup toasted slivered almonds
  (see page 16)

ꜱ●꜕ DIRECTIONS

1. Line a jelly-roll pan with aluminum foil, smoothing out any wrinkles. Coat foil with nonstick cooking spray.

2. Stir together sugar, corn syrup, and water in a large saucepan. Heat over medium heat until it reaches a boil, then boil gently until it reaches 248°F (firm-ball stage).

3. Meanwhile, beat egg whites in a clean grease-free bowl on medium speed until soft peaks form. Add salt and continue beating until stiff, but not dry, peaks form.

4. As soon as the syrup reaches 248°F, pour about half of it (you can eyeball this) over egg whites in a thin stream, avoiding the sides of the bowl and the beaters, beating egg whites all the while. Keep egg whites beating as you proceed.

5. Cook remaining syrup to 275°F (soft-crack stage), then pour in a thin stream over egg white mixture. Beat until cool, stiff, and glossy, then beat in extracts. Fold in peel and nuts, then drop by tablespoonfuls onto the prepared pan. The mixture will be sticky; use another spoon to scrape the candy off the table-spoon. Allow to sit until cooled and firm, about 30 minutes.

Angel Food Candy

>●< **HOLIDAY** *Christmas*

>●< **TYPE** *Bar candy*   >●< **HABITAT** *United States*

>●< **DESCRIPTION** *Angel food candy has the flavor of caramelized sugar in a crunchy, chewy form. It is made in a pan, then broken apart into randomly sized chunks, which are then dipped in chocolate.*

>●< **FIELD NOTES** *This is an old-fashioned American candy. Sometimes it is also called sponge candy or honeycomb candy, as its appearance, due to the action of the baking soda and vinegar, is porous. It is easy to make and kids like to see the transformation when the baking soda and vinegar are added. I have no idea why it was named "angel food"—maybe because it is light and airy and wouldn't weigh angels down from their flying duties.*

>●< **LIFESPAN** *1 week refrigerated in airtight container in single layers separated by waxed or parchment paper*

Yield: *about 60 chunks*

⊳●⊲ INGREDIENTS

I cup granulated sugar
I cup dark corn syrup
I tablespoon baking soda

I tablespoon cider vinegar
1¹/₂ pounds semisweet chocolate, finely
chopped

⊳●⊲ DIRECTIONS

1. Line a 9-inch baking pan with aluminum foil so that foil overhangs by a few inches on all sides; butter the foil generously.

2. Stir together sugar and corn syrup in a large deep saucepan. Bring to a boil over medium heat and cook to 300°F (hard-crack stage). Watch carefully to prevent it from boiling over. Immediately remove from heat.

3. Add baking soda and vinegar and whisk vigorously to combine thoroughly. The mixture will lighten and foam up. Quickly scrape into prepared pan and place on rack to cool completely.

4. Unmold by pulling foil up and out of pan; peel off foil. Cut into chunks 1 to 2 inches across.

5. Line a jelly-roll pan with aluminum foil, smoothing out any wrinkles. Coat foil with nonstick cooking spray.

6. Temper chocolate according to the directions on page 14. Dip chunks into chocolate one at a time until completely coated, using your fingers, 2 forks, or chocolate dipping tools. Remove from chocolate, let excess chocolate drip back into pot, and place angel food back on foil. Chill until firm, about 30 minutes.

Candy Tidbits

Make sure to whisk in the baking soda thoroughly or else you will have pockets of it here and there, which would be most unpalatable. Also, you don't have to dip the candy in chocolate if you prefer not to—this is delicious as is!

"Barley" Sugar Toys

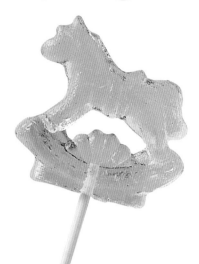

⟡ **HOLIDAY** *Christmas*

⟡ **TYPE** *Molded candy*   ⟡ **HABITAT** *United States and Germany*

⟡ **DESCRIPTION** *The look of these lollipops depends on the molds used to make them. They should look like small toys made out of crystal-clear (although often colored) candy. You can color and flavor them any way you like, but I suggest one flavor and color per batch. One batch can be made and cooled within half an hour, so you can make subsequent batches fairly quickly.*

⟡ **FIELD NOTES** *John Wright lollipop molds, which I used to test this recipe, are available seasonally from Williams-Sonoma. Mine feature a rocking reindeer, a wreath, a toy soldier, and other holiday shapes. These candies are often referred to as clear toy candies, and were introduced to this country by German immigrants who settled in Pennsylvania in 1772. The original candy was made from barley sugar, which was cheaper to use at the time. The addition of cream of tartar lends a slight sourness that mimics the flavor of barley sugar. This recipe fills the set of eight molds that I have. Other molds might result in a different yield.*

⟡ **LIFESPAN** *1 month at room temperature, individually wrapped*

Yield: *8 sugar toys*

Tools: *Cast-metal candy molds • Eight 4-inch lollipop sticks • 8 clear candy bags •*
8 decorative twist ties or pieces of ribbon

⋑●⋐ INGREDIENTS

1 cup plus 2 tablespoons granulated sugar
2 tablespoons light corn syrup
¹/₄ cup water
Heaping ¹/₄ teaspoon cream of tartar

1 teaspoon lemon oil, lime oil, peppermint
oil, or cherry flavoring
Yellow, green, or red liquid food coloring

⋑●⋐ DIRECTIONS

1. Wipe molds with a clean soft dishcloth to remove any dust. Assemble
molds according to manufacturer's
instructions.

2. Stir sugar, corn syrup, water, and cream
of tartar together in a small saucepan.
Bring to a boil over medium-high heat,
swirling the pot once or twice. Bring
mixture to 300°F (hard-crack stage)
and immediately remove from heat.
Allow bubbling to subside, then add
flavoring and several drops of food
coloring and swirl to incorporate.

3. Slowly pour mixture into molds, filling
about halfway, then go back and top
them off. Take care as mixture nears
the top, as it can overflow easily.

4. Allow candies to set for about 15
seconds, then insert lollipop sticks.
Allow to harden until the outsides of
the molds are barely warm. Carefully
unmold candies per manufacturer's
instructions. (This usually involves
simply separating the two halves of the
mold and gently pulling the lollipops
out by the stick. If they don't come
apart easily, cool them further, then
use the tip of a knife to gently pry the
molds apart and pry the lollipops out
of their molds.) Cool completely, then
place in candy bags and seal with a
twist tie.

New Orleans–Style Pralines

⋙●⋘ **HOLIDAY** *Christmas*

⋙●⋘ **TYPE** *Drop candy*   ⋙●⋘ **HABITAT** *Southern United States*

⋙●⋘ **DESCRIPTION** *If you like brown sugar and pecans, there is no better way to get them into your mouth than via this candy. Pralines (pronounced prah-leens) are a simple mixture of brown sugar, butter, and milk, cooked and stirred until somewhat creamy, somewhat crumbly—with a bunch of pecans thrown in for good measure.*

⋙●⋘ **FIELD NOTES** *Pralines are very popular down South and, as with any down home–style candy, practically every cook will have a different version, many of which have been handed down through the generations. In fact, pralines probably date back to the mid-1700s. Some current recipes use all brown sugar, or heavy cream; some call for chopped pecans, and some leave them whole. Probably the biggest difference is that there are camps that believe pralines should be creamy and others that think a crumbly brown sugary texture is "traditional." It probably depends on how your grandma made them! These lean toward crumbly, because they are easier to make and just as delectable.*

⋙●⋘ **LIFESPAN** *1 month at room temperature in airtight container in single layers separated by waxed or parchment paper*

Yield: *about 24 pralines*

INGREDIENTS

1 cup granulated sugar
1 cup packed light brown sugar
$^1/_2$ cup evaporated milk
4 tablespoons ($^1/_2$ stick) unsalted butter, cut into pieces

2 teaspoons vanilla extract
$1^1/_2$ cups pecan halves, coarsely chopped

DIRECTIONS

1. Line a jelly-roll pan with aluminum foil, smoothing out any wrinkles. Coat foil with nonstick cooking spray.

2. Combine the granulated sugar, brown sugar, and milk in a saucepan and stir to moisten. Cook over medium heat, bringing to a simmer. Cook until it reaches 235°F (soft-ball stage).

3. Remove from heat and add butter pieces. Allow mixture to sit for 1 minute to soften butter, then stir in butter and add vanilla and nuts, stirring quickly but gently just until the mixture loses its sheen and starts to thicken.

4. Immediately drop generous tablespoons of the mixture onto the prepared pan, spacing the candies apart. The pralines should be about 2 inches wide.

5. The pralines will firm up almost immediately. Once they are cool and firm they are ready to serve.

Candy Tidbits

Feel free to experiment with dark brown sugar for a more pronounced molasses-like taste. Also, pralines can be gussied up by pressing one whole pecan half onto the top of each one while still soft.

White Christmas

≫●≪ **HOLIDAY** *Christmas*

≫●≪ **TYPE** *Bar candy*   ≫●≪ **HABITAT** *Australia*

≫●≪ **DESCRIPTION** *This candy has a very unusual taste and texture due to copha, which is an Australian shortening derived from coconuts. It is the binder in this recipe for grated coconut, milk powder, crisped rice cereal, sugar, and dried fruit.*

≫●≪ **FIELD NOTES** *I asked Kim de la Villefromoy, an Australian friend of mine and owner of Chef Revival clothing, if there were any candies that I should include in this book, and he immediately said, "White Christmas, of course." I soon came to understand that all Aussies know this candy and that it belonged in this collection. You do need copha; typical American shortening will not suffice. It is inexpensive and can be ordered from the Australian Catalogue Company (see Resources).*

≫●≪ **LIFESPAN** *2 weeks at room temperature in single layers separated by waxed or parchment paper*

Yield: *25 candies*

⋙●⋘ INGREDIENTS

8 ounces copha
1 cup confectioners' sugar
1 cup crisped rice cereal (such as Rice Krispies)
1 cup unsweetened grated coconut

1 cup nonfat dried milk powder
1 cup candied cherries, quartered
$^1/_2$ cup diced candied pineapple
$^1/_2$ cup golden raisins

⋙●⋘ DIRECTIONS

1. Coat a 9-inch square baking pan with nonstick cooking spray.

2. Melt copha in a small saucepan over medium heat.

3. Meanwhile, toss together remaining ingredients in a large bowl.

4. Pour copha over dry mixture and mix with your hands until thoroughly combined. (You can use a spoon or spatula, but I find my hands are more efficient with this candy.)

5. Scrape mixture into prepared pan and pat down as firmly as possible.

6. Refrigerate until set, about 30 minutes. Cut into 25 squares (5 x 5).

Candy Tidbits

You can, of course, play around with the fruit. I have used dried apricots, candied ginger, dark raisins, and even nuts. To really gussy it up, you could drizzle white chocolate over the top, but these are pretty sweet already.

Glazed Chestnuts

🍬 **HOLIDAY** *Christmas*

🍬 **TYPE** *Hand-formed candy*   🍬 **HABITAT** *France and Italy*

🍬 **DESCRIPTION** *Cooked chestnuts are simmered in a sugar syrup, then dried and simmered again to produce tender chestnuts with a shiny sugar glaze.*

🍬 **FIELD NOTES** *Chestnuts are a fall crop, and one way of preserving them, in a sweet fashion, is to glaze them. Various parts of Europe feature this confection, particularly at Christmastime. I have started with cooked chestnuts to make this super-easy. They really vary by size. Look for very plump chestnuts, which is easy to see if they are in a glass jar. If they are canned, you get what you get. Either way, do not use the kind packed in syrup.*

🍬 **LIFESPAN** *1 week at room temperature in airtight container; 1 month refrigerated*

Yield: *about 30 confections, depending on size*

❧●❧ INGREDIENTS

1 cup granulated sugar
1 cup light corn syrup
$^1/_2$ cup water
1 pound cooked, dry chestnuts

$^1/_2$ teaspoon vanilla extract
30 small fluted paper cups or small square candy wrappers or cellophane

❧●❧ DIRECTIONS

1. Coat a cooling rack with nonstick cooking spray and place over a jelly-roll pan.

2. Stir together sugar, corn syrup, and water in a large saucepan. Bring to a boil over medium-high heat and simmer until sugar dissolves, swirling pan once or twice.

3. Add chestnuts and simmer over medium heat for 10 minutes. Do not boil hard, as the nuts may fall apart.

4. Remove chestnuts from syrup with a slotted spoon and place on prepared rack to dry overnight or up to 24 hours. Reserve syrup in pan, covered.

5. Reheat syrup in pan, add chestnuts and vanilla, and stir to combine. Simmer over medium heat for about 5 minutes or until syrup is very thick and chest-nuts are thickly coated in glaze. Cool to just warm.

6. Remove chestnuts again using a slotted spoon and allow to dry completely on rack. Place individual chestnuts in paper cups or wrap in candy wrappers or cellophane.

Candy Tidbits

If you want to use fresh chestnuts, cut a small x in the bottom of each shell. Place chestnuts in a large pan and cover with water. Bring to a boil over high heat; turn heat down to medium, cover, and simmer until nuts are tender when pierced with a sharp knife tip, about 30 minutes. Drain and cool, then peel nuts and proceed.

Apricot Candies (*Mebos*)

HOLIDAY *Christmas*

TYPE *Hand-formed candy*   **HABITAT** *South Africa*

DESCRIPTION *These are very sweet cooked apricot confections. You start with dried apricots and simply cook them down with sugar and spread into a pan to cool before cutting and rolling in sugar.*

FIELD NOTES *Many cultures develop cooked fruit candies as a way to preserve bumper crops—and to have something sweet on the table! These hail from my newfound friend Alicia Wilkinson, who teaches cooking in South Africa. She responded to an e-mail query and graciously shared some of her families' recipes. Research that I conducted found that sometimes the apricots are cooked in a brine, but here they are sweet through and through.*

LIFESPAN *1 month refrigerated in airtight container in single layers separated by waxed or parchment paper*

Yield: *80 confections*

❧●❧ INGREDIENTS

2 1/4 cups dried apricots
2 cups water

2 3/4 cups granulated sugar, plus more for rolling
80 small fluted paper cups

❧●❧ DIRECTIONS

1. Lightly oil the inside of a 9 x 13-inch baking pan with canola oil.

2. Cook apricots and water in a medium-size saucepan over medium heat until mixture simmers. Turn heat to low and simmer for about 10 minutes. The apricots will soften and almost all of the liquid will be absorbed.

3. Drain apricots, reserving remaining liquid. Place apricots in a food processor fitted with a metal blade and process until a smooth paste forms. Scrape paste back into saucepan and add 3 tablespoons of the reserved cooking liquid. Discard the rest. Add 2 3/4 cups sugar and stir to combine.

4. Cook mixture over medium heat for about 15 minutes, stirring frequently. The mixture will first darken and become less opaque. Eventually it will become a little foamy and very thick. Cook to 245°F (firm-ball stage). Scrape mixture into prepared pan, smoothing the top with an offset spatula.

5. Allow to sit at cool room temperature for about 4 hours or until set. Cut into 80 tiny rectangles (10 x 8). Remove pieces with a sharp knife and offset spatula. They will be sticky and not really hold their shape, which is okay. Use your fingers and palms to form them into rough barrel shapes and roll them in sugar. Place them in the paper cups.

Turkish Delight (*Lokum*)

🍬 **HOLIDAY** *Christmas, Shekar Bayrami (Turkish Holiday of Candy)*

🍬 **TYPE** *Bar candy*   🍬 **HABITAT** *Turkey*

🍬 **DESCRIPTION** *This confection has an unusual floral flavor from the orange flower water, and an intriguing texture from the gelatin and cornstarch. Pistachios give it a bit of crunch. Note that this candy needs a ripening period overnight in the refrigerator.*

🍬 **FIELD NOTES** *To the American palate, lokum might be considered an acquired taste, but in Turkey, hardly a celebration goes by without an offering of Turkish Delight. This ancient confection dates back to the Ottoman Empire. The story goes that a wealthy sultan requested that his confectioner invent a sweet that would win back the love of his favorite concubine from his harem. The candy came to the West in the nineteenth century, when a traveler brought some to England and dubbed it Turkish Delight. Turkey has a holiday dedicated to candy called Shekar Bayrami, which ends the month of fasting for Ramadan. Many candies are served, including lokum, as well as candied nuts and marzipan.*

🍬 **LIFESPAN** *1 week at room temperature in airtight container in single layers separated by waxed or parchment paper*

Yield: *64 squares*

●◄ INGREDIENTS

4 cups sugar

4 cups water

1 tablespoon lemon juice

¼ cup unflavored gelatin

1 cup cornstarch

1 teaspoon cream of tartar

2 tablespoons orange flower water or rose water

1 drop red liquid food coloring

1 drop yellow liquid food coloring

⅔ cup chopped toasted pistachios (see page 16)

Topping:

½ cup confectioners' sugar

½ cup cornstarch

●◄ DIRECTIONS

1. Lightly oil a 9-inch square baking pan with canola oil.

2. Stir together sugar, 1½ cups water, and lemon juice in a large heavy saucepan. Bring to a boil over medium heat, swirling the pan occasionally until the mixture reaches 240°F (soft-ball stage), about 8 minutes.

3. Meanwhile, stir together ½ cup cold water and gelatin in a small bowl; it will be thick. Let sit 5 minutes to soften, then stir in remaining 2 cups water (make it hot from the tap) to begin to dissolve gelatin.

4. Also while sugar is boiling, whisk cornstarch and cream of tartar together in a large bowl. Slowly whisk in gelatin mixture.

5. When sugar syrup is ready, slowly whisk in the gelatin-cornstarch mixture and continue to cook over medium heat. It should simmer gently until it thickens and clears, about 3 minutes; it will look like raw egg white.

6. Immediately stir in orange flower water, food coloring, and nuts, then pour into the prepared pan. Cool to room temperature, cover with plastic wrap, then refrigerate overnight.

7. For the topping, whisk together confectioners' sugar and cornstarch in a medium bowl. Cut candy into 64 squares (8 x 8), then toss squares in topping mixture to coat thoroughly.

Caramelized Milk Candies (Tejas)

☙●❦ **HOLIDAY** *Christmas*

☙●❦ **TYPE** *Hand-formed candy*   ☙●❦ **HABITAT** *Peru*

☙●❦ **DESCRIPTION** *These feature* manjar blanco *(also called* dulce de leche, cajita, *or* arquipe, *among other terms, depending on where you are from), which is a caramelized sweetened milk. That ingredient, combined with pecans and semisweet chocolate, make a very tasty and different chocolate candy.*

☙●❦ **FIELD NOTES** *David Jesson from Peru came through with loads of information on South American candies. He explained to me how* manjar blanco *is used in various preparations from candies like this to simply being spread on bread. You have to make the* manjar blanco *first, and some say the technique of boiling the sealed can may be dangerous. Just make sure the can has no bulges and is airtight. An alternative approach to the widespread practice described in the instructions is to punch a tiny hole in the top of the can and keep the water just below the top of the can. This process will take longer, and it is hard to gauge when the mixture will be done, but 7 hours is a good guess. You need to plan ahead anyway because the recipe as is takes 5 hours. Tejas, by the way, means "Texas" as well as "tiles." Some similar candies in Peru are prepared to resemble curved roof tiles; this version looks more like little nuggets.*

☙●❦ **LIFESPAN** *1 month refrigerated in airtight container*

Yield: *60* tejas

▷●◁ INGREDIENTS

One 14-ounce can sweetened condensed milk

120 toasted whole pecan halves (see page 16; about 1³/₄ cups)

8 ounces couverture semisweet chocolate (see page 10), finely chopped

▷●◁ DIRECTIONS

1. Make sure can has no bulges or dents. Remove paper label from can. Place can in saucepan deep enough so that water can cover the top. Cover the can with water, cover the saucepan, and bring to a boil over medium-high heat, then adjust heat so there is a constant simmer and cook for 5 hours (yes, 5 hours). Replace water if it dips below the bottom of the can.

2. Remove from heat and let can cool in water, which could take an hour. Remove from water and wipe can clean and dry. Open can; the milk should look dark like caramel and be thick enough to scoop, like peanut butter. If it is not thick enough, try refrigerating overnight.

3. Line a jelly-roll pan with aluminum foil, shiny side up, smoothing out any wrinkles, or line the pan with a piece of acetate. Use a teaspoon to scoop up a tiny bit of the *manjar blanco* and sandwich it between two pecans. Repeat with all the nuts and place on prepared pan.

4. Temper chocolate according to the directions on page 14. Dip filled pecans one at a time in the melted chocolate until completely coated, using your fingers, 2 forks, or chocolate dipping tools. Allow excess chocolate to drip back into the pot. Place *tejas* carefully on the lined pan. Refrigerate until firm, but serve at room temperature.

Candy Tidbits

Many of the chocolate candies in this book are sturdy enough to mail, but I always take care to keep them cool by packing them along with a freezer pack.

Coconut Candies
(Beijinho de Coco)

➽●◀ HOLIDAY *Christmas*

➽●◀ TYPE *Hand-formed candy*   **➽●◀ HABITAT** *Brazil*

➽●◀ DESCRIPTION *Sweetened condensed milk makes these candies super easy to prepare, and quick too. A simple combination of the sweetened milk, coconut, coconut milk, and egg yolks is cooked and rolled into balls. Each one has a whole clove, which is mostly for decoration but also subtly perfumes the candy. Remove it before eating.*

➽●◀ FIELD NOTES *Egg yolks and cloves are very common ingredients in South American candies, as is sweet, thick milk, which our sweetened condensed milk duplicates. The coconut milk can be found in Asian grocery stores and large supermarkets; it is not the same as the very sweet cream of coconut. You want 100 percent coconut milk with no added sugar. The original recipes I found called for freshly grated coconut. I find that a mixture of unsweetened grated coconut and sweetened flaked coconut gives the right result, without you needing to crack a coconut at home.*

➽●◀ LIFESPAN *1 week at room temperature in airtight container in single layers separated by waxed or parchment paper*

Yield: *40 candies*

▷●◁ INGREDIENTS

One 14-ounce can sweetened condensed
  milk
¹/₂ cup coconut milk
³/₄ cup unsweetened grated coconut
¹/₄ cup sweetened flaked coconut

3 large egg yolks
Granulated sugar
40 whole cloves
40 small fluted paper cups

▷●◁ DIRECTIONS

1. Coat a 9-inch square baking pan with
   nonstick cooking spray.

2. Whisk together condensed milk,
   coconut milk, both types of coconut,
   and egg yolks in a large saucepan.
   Cook over medium heat at a gentle
   simmer, stirring constantly, until
   mixture thickens and you can see
   the bottom of the pan for a moment
   if you draw a spoon through the mixture. This will take about 5 minutes.

3. Scrape mixture into pan, spreading into
   an even layer using an offset spatula,
   and cool to room temperature, then
   refrigerate until firm, about 2 hours.

4. Place granulated sugar in a medium-
   size bowl. Scoop mixture using a teaspoon or small ice cream scoop and
   roll into ³/₄-inch balls. Roll them in
   sugar. Insert one clove into each candy
   and place candy in a paper cup.

Egg Yolk Nougat (*Turron de Yema*)

🍬 **HOLIDAY** *Christmas*

🍬 **TYPE** *Bar candy*   🍬 **HABITAT** *Spain*

🍬 **DESCRIPTION** *This particular nougat is made with ground almonds, cinnamon, and lemon zest. It is enriched with egg yolks that are added to the cooked sugar syrup. It does not look or taste like the nougats we are used to seeing in the United States; it resembles more of a nut shortbread.*

🍬 **FIELD NOTES** *Various types of nougats, most featuring nuts, are popular in Spain. They are offered to guests and family at the holidays, often at the end of the meal with coffee or liqueurs. There is* alicante, *which is a hard nougat similar to what we think of as a nut brittle, and* jijona, *which is a soft nougat, more like the one on page 158, which is also popular in France and Italy. However, the production of these traditional confections is strictly controlled by a governing body, so even if we make an* alicante-*like nougat, it cannot legally be sold as such in Spain unless we are certified to do so! But we can certainly make these treats at home. I chose this one with egg yolks because it is very different and yet still representative of Spanish cuisine.*

🍬 **LIFESPAN** *2 weeks at room temperature in airtight container in single layers separated by waxed or parchment paper*

Yield: *64 nougats*

INGREDIENTS

2 ¹/₃ cups slivered almonds, finely ground
  to a powder
6 large egg yolks
1 ²/₃ cups granulated sugar

¹/₂ cup water
1 teaspoon lemon zest
¹/₈ teaspoon cinnamon

DIRECTIONS

1. Line a 9-inch square baking pan with aluminum foil so that foil overhangs by a few inches on all sides. Smooth out any wrinkles and butter foil generously.

2. Fold almonds and egg yolks together to make a very thick paste.

3. Stir sugar and water together in a medium-size deep saucepan. Bring to a boil over medium heat until it just begins to turn a very light golden color.

4. Immediately remove from heat. Stir in almond mixture, lemon zest, and cinnamon. The mixture will be very thick, but keep stirring until combined.

5. Place back over medium heat and cook, stirring constantly, until almonds begin to smell fragrant and mixture begins to turn a light amber brown, about 5 minutes.

6. Scrape into prepared pan. Quickly rinse hands with cold water, shake off excess water, and pat nougat down into a flat even layer. Place pan on rack to cool until slightly warm. Score 64 pieces (8 x 8) and let cool completely. Unmold by pulling foil up and out of pan; peel off foil. Cut candy along score lines.

Candy Tidbits

You will get the best results if the almonds are very, very finely ground. They should be powdery and without much texture. This is best accomplished in a food processor fitted with a metal blade, pulsing on and off until you get the results that you want.

Italian Nougat (*Torrone*)

>●< **HOLIDAY** *Christmas*

>●< **TYPE** *Bar candy*   >●< **HABITAT** *Italy*

>●< **DESCRIPTION** *This classic nougat is chewy, sweet, and filled with nuts and dried fruit. It looks like a mosaic when cut.*

>●< **FIELD NOTES** *Nougat is very popular in Italy at Christmastime, but the confection is also popular in France. The filling should contain nuts, but you can vary the additions—try pistachios, candied lemon peel, dried cranberries, or hazelnuts. The rice or wafer paper (which is made from flour) is a confectionery product that can be found at Sweet Celebrations (see Resources). For the honey, try to find unfiltered, raw honey. There are those nougat connoisseurs who say the recipe will not work with pasteurized honey. The only trick with this recipe is to have the egg whites whipped to the proper point when the sugar syrup is ready. And last but not least, I highly recommend a stand mixer, as this mixture is very thick and there are steps that need to happen simultaneously; a stand mixer will free up your hands.*

>●< **LIFESPAN** *1 month at room temperature in airtight container*

Yield: *64 nougats*

❧●❧ INGREDIENTS

Two 8-inch squares of rice or wafer paper
I cup peeled hazelnuts, coarsely chopped
²/₃ cup dried cherries
¹/₂ cup blanched sliced almonds, toasted
  (see page 16)
¹/₂ cup diced candied orange peel
2 cups granulated sugar
I cup light corn syrup
¹/₂ cup honey
¹/₄ cup water

Pinch of salt
2 large egg whites
¹/₈ teaspoon cream of tartar
I teaspoon vanilla extract
I teaspoon almond extract
¹/₄ cup (¹/₂ stick) unsalted butter, at room
  temperature, cut into pieces
64 small square candy wrappers or
  cellophane

❧●❧ DIRECTIONS

1. Line the bottom of an 8-inch square baking pan with a piece of rice paper cut to fit; butter the sides well. Have second piece of paper in reserve.

2. Toss the nuts, fruit, and orange peel together in a bowl.

3. Stir together granulated sugar, corn syrup, honey, water, and salt in a large saucepan. Bring to a boil over high heat, swirling the pot once or twice to help dissolve sugar.

4. Meanwhile, in a large, clean grease-free bowl with an electric mixer on medium speed, beat egg whites until frothy. Add cream of tartar and beat on high speed until soft peaks form.

5. Cook syrup to 260°F (hard-ball stage). Immediately remove from heat, and with mixer running, carefully pour about one-fourth of the syrup over the egg whites, avoiding the sides of the bowl and the beaters. Quickly put pot back over heat and continue to cook syrup. Meanwhile, beat egg whites on high speed until meringue becomes thick and glossy.

6. When remaining syrup reaches 300°F (hard-crack stage), carefully pour it over meringue, beating all the while until very stiff, about 5 minutes.

7. Beat in extracts and butter. The meringue will repel the butter at first. Keep beating, or stir in by hand. Beat in nut-fruit mixture; this is best accomplished by hand with a rubber spatula.

8. Immediately scrape into prepared pan and pat down with damp fingers so it is as level as possible. Place second piece of rice or wafer paper on top and weigh down as evenly as possible for about 3 hours. (You can use another pan filled with canned food to weigh down candy.) Cool completely.

9. To unmold nougat from the pan, place a piece of parchment or waxed paper on work surface, run a buttered knife around the edges of the candy, and flip the pan over onto parchment paper. Rap the pan firmly on the table to unmold candy. You might have to wedge an offset spatula beneath the nougat to ease it out. Use a buttered sharp knife, pressing it straight down but not dragging it through, to cut candy into 64 pieces (8 x 8). Or, rinse a knife with water and try the same cutting technique. Wrap candies individually in wrappers.

Panforte di Siena

🍬 **HOLIDAY** *Christmas*   🍬 **TYPE** *Bar candy*

🍬 **HABITAT** *Italy*

🍬 **DESCRIPTION** *This very easy-to-make treat combines hazelnuts, almonds, figs, apricots, cherries, candied orange zest, cocoa powder, and spices with honey to make a dense, chewy, round "cake" that is cut into thin pieces for serving.*

🍬 **FIELD NOTES** Panforte *means "strong bread," and yet this dish is experienced as a sweet, chewy confection, hence its inclusion here. The Tuscan town of Siena has become famous for it (some accounts date it back to 1205). Some versions contain coriander, which you may add if you like. Serve it with a glass of Vin Santo, as they often do in Italy.*

🍬 **LIFESPAN** *1 week at room temperature in airtight container; 1 month refrigerated*

Yield: *12 slices*

▷●◁ INGREDIENTS

2 cups toasted, skinned hazelnuts (see page 16), coarsely chopped

2 cups toasted, skinned whole almonds (see page 16), coarsely chopped

²/₃ cup finely chopped Calimyrna figs

²/₃ cup finely chopped dried cherries

¹/₂ cup finely chopped apricots

¹/₂ cup diced candied orange peel

1¹/₂ cups all-purpose flour

2 tablespoons unsweetened Dutch-processed cocoa powder

1 teaspoon cinnamon

1 teaspoon ground ginger

¹/₂ teaspoon white pepper

¹/₄ teaspoon nutmeg

1¹/₄ cups granulated sugar

²/₃ cup honey

Confectioners' sugar or unsweetened Dutch-processed cocoa powder for dusting

▷●◁ DIRECTIONS

1. Preheat oven to 325°F. Line a 10 x 2-inch round cake pan with a parchment circle and coat parchment and pan's sides with nonstick cooking spray.

2. Toss together nuts, fruit, orange peel, flour, cocoa powder, and spices in a large bowl.

3. Stir sugar and honey together in a medium-size saucepan. Bring to a boil over medium heat and boil gently for 2 minutes.

4. Remove from heat and pour over dry ingredients. Mix well; the mixture will be very thick and heavy. Using your hands is easiest; just make sure everything is evenly combined. Scrape into the prepared pan, patting top smooth with your hands.

5. Bake for about 32 minutes or until toothpick inserted in center comes out just clean. The top might begin to color, but it is hard to see because it is so dark to begin with. Cool on rack for 5 minutes, then unmold, peel off parchment, and cool completely.

6. To store, double wrap in plastic wrap, then wrap in foil and place in an airtight container. Dust with confectioners' sugar or cocoa powder just before serving.

Candy Tidbits

The nuts and fruits can be varied: try walnuts, dates, lemon peel, and prunes, for starters. Just stick with the same total amounts.

Chocolate-Covered
Caramelized Almonds

⟫●⟪ HOLIDAY *Christmas*

⟫●⟪ TYPE *Hand-formed candy*   **⟫●⟪ HABITAT** *United States*

⟫●⟪ DESCRIPTION *These candies are very sophisticated—whole almonds are coated with caramelized sugar, then coated in tempered chocolate and dusted with your choice of cocoa powder or confectioners' sugar.*

⟫●⟪ FIELD NOTES *I list these as a Christmas candy because they make elegant gifts— for teachers, hosts and hostesses, long-distance family and friends, and to offer last-minute visitors. To make them ultra-fancy, divide the mixture into thirds and toss one part with Dutch-processed cocoa powder, another with natural cocoa powder, and the rest with confectioners' sugar. Be careful not to overcook the mixture in Step 4 of the directions. If all of the sugar reliquefies, it will puddle around the nuts when you scrape them onto the pan and make more of a brittle. You want the nuts to be individually coated with caramel and remain as round in shape as possible.*

⟫●⟪ LIFESPAN *1 month at room temperature in airtight container*

Yield: *about 30 servings (of about a half dozen almonds each)*

✿ INGREDIENTS

1³/₄ cups granulated sugar
³/₄ cup water
3¹/₄ cups whole natural almonds
12 ounces couverture bitterweet
  chocolate (see page 10), finely chopped

1¹/₂ cups unsweetened Dutch-processed
  cocoa powder (or equal parts Dutch
  cocoa powder, natural cocoa powder,
  and confectioners' sugar, kept separated)

✿ DIRECTIONS

1. Line a jelly-roll pan with aluminum foil, smoothing out any wrinkles. Coat foil with nonstick cooking spray.

2. Stir sugar and water together in a large saucepan or a nonstick wok. Bring to a boil over high heat and cook until sugar dissolves. Add almonds and continue to cook over high heat, stirring occasionally. Watch the sugar syrup. At first it will be fluid with small bubbles as it boils. Gradually bubbles will get larger and syrup will begin to color and caramelize.

3. When syrup begins to thicken, start stirring constantly with a large wooden spoon or spatula, tossing the nuts within the syrup. Keep stirring; the mixture will eventually turn foamy, about 10 minutes total. Keep stirring and the syrup will crystallize and turn sugary. Keep tossing the nuts within the mixture so that they become evenly coated.

4. Turn the heat down to medium-high and watch very carefully. The sugary mixture will begin to reliquefy within a few minutes and be an amber color. Keep stirring as sugar reliquefies and coats nuts with a mostly shiny caramel. There might still be a few sugary crystals here and there—that's okay.

5. Immediately scrape nuts onto the prepared pan and quickly separate as many individual nuts as possible. The mixture will harden quickly. Don't worry if a few nuts clump into small groupings.

6. Let nuts sit at room temperature for about 30 minutes until they are hard and cool. Meanwhile, temper chocolate according to the directions on page 14.

7. Place nuts in a very large bowl, using your fingers to separate any nuts that remain clumped together. Pour about one-fourth of the chocolate over nuts and stir to evenly coat; keep stirring until it begins to harden around nuts. Add another fourth of the chocolate and stir some more, again allowing the chocolate to coat the nuts. Add more chocolate only if necessary for even coating.

8. Divide nuts between bowls if you are using more than one coating. Quickly, while the chocolate is still a little soft with some tackiness, add one of the cocoa powders and/or confectioners' sugar and stir some more. Keep stirring until each nut is coated. When you think they are done, put down the spoon and use your hands to shake the bowl front and back with a rounded motion so that the nuts tumble over one another. Keep doing this and they will take on a bit more coating.

Burnt Almonds *(Brente Mandler)*

HOLIDAY *Christmas*

TYPE *Hand-formed candy*   **HABITAT** *Norway*

DESCRIPTION *Toasted almonds are combined with caramelized sugar to produce a crunchy nut brittle. While you could leave the brittle in a sheet and break off hunks, these are meant to be more like individual nuts, or small clusters, coated with crunchy caramel glaze. These might sound similar to the Chocolate-Covered Caramelized Almonds on page 162, but they are made by different techniques and actually taste quite different. This recipe has no chocolate and cocoa, and the sugar is cooked to a different texture.*

FIELD NOTES *A few authentic Norwegian Christmas recipes came into my hands through Enge Berit from Oslo. I immediately recognized the similarities between this recipe and others from various parts of the world. Nut brittles are found in the United States, Europe, Russia, the Middle East, and elsewhere, so I knew I wanted to include a recipe for this popular confection.*

LIFESPAN *1 month at room temperature in airtight container in single layers separated by waxed or parchment paper*

Yield: *50 clusters or 1¹/₂ pounds*

⊱●⊰ INGREDIENTS

2 cups granulated sugar

1 cup water

2 cups toasted whole blanched almonds (see page 16)

⊱●⊰ DIRECTIONS

1. Lightly oil a jelly-roll pan and two forks with canola oil; set aside forks but place pan in oven.

2. Preheat oven to 200°F with pan in oven. Stir sugar and water together in a large saucepan. Bring to a boil over medium-high heat and cook until it is a light golden color.

3. Remove from heat and immediately stir in almonds until coated with caramel. Quickly remove the pan from the oven, set on a cooling rack, and quickly scrape mixture onto prepared pan. Immediately use oiled forks to separate nuts into individual nuts or little clusters. You must work fast before the caramel hardens. Allow nut brittle to cool and harden at room temperature.

Candy Tidbits

Other nuts may be substituted, but almonds are traditional. Heating the pan allows you some extra time to separate the nuts or clusters.

Pastel Butter Mints

❧●❧ **HOLIDAY** *Weddings*

❧●❧ **TYPE** *Hand-formed candy*   ❧●❧ **HABITAT** *United States*

❧●❧ **DESCRIPTION** *These minty candies are soft, with a creamy inside and a firm exterior that is gained simply through drying at room temperature. They can be made with or without molds.*

❧●❧ **FIELD NOTES** *You know those little mints you see at restaurants at the cash register? These look and taste exactly like them. They are very easy to make and can be set out in bowls on tables at a wedding for an easy, inexpensive favor. Note that these need to dry overnight.*

❧●❧ **LIFESPAN** *2 weeks at room temperature in airtight container in single layers separated by waxed or parchment paper*

Yield: *about 160 tiny mints*

✎●✎ INGREDIENTS

4 1/2 to 4 3/4 cups confectioners' sugar
1/2 cup (1 stick) unsalted butter, at room
temperature, cut into pieces
2 tablespoons heavy cream or evaporated
milk

Peppermint oil (such as LorAnn's)
Green, red, or yellow liquid food coloring

✎●✎ DIRECTIONS

1. Line a jelly-roll pan with aluminum foil, smoothing out any wrinkles.

2. In a large bowl with an electric mixer on low to medium speed, beat 4½ cups confectioners' sugar, butter, and cream until very soft and creamy, about 3 minutes. Once the sugar is incorporated with the other ingredients, you can beat on high speed until the desired texture is achieved. Beat in 2 to 3 drops of peppermint oil and 1 to 2 drops of food coloring, then adjust to your taste. You want a pronounced mint flavor and a pale color.

3. Pick up a piece and roll between your palms; it should not be sticky. Add more confectioners' sugar if necessary.

4. Knead the mixture until smooth. Roll pieces into ropes about ½ inch around. Cut small mints off the rope, each about ⅔ inch long.

5. Spread mints onto prepared pan so that they are not touching, and allow to dry at least overnight. Shake pan 2 or 3 times during drying period to allow all sides to be exposed to air.

Candy Tidbits

You can roll out the mints like cookie dough to a ½-inch thickness and cut out shapes with small cookie cutters. Or you can press the mixture into rubber molds. Roll small pieces in superfine sugar first, then press into mold, scraping off any excess along the edges of mold, and pop out of mold to dry. You can see all three in the photo. Also, you can divide the dough after it is flavored and color it various pastel colors so you get three colors out of one batch.

Cream Cheese Rosettes

🍬 **HOLIDAY** *Weddings*

🍬 **TYPE** *Piped candy*   🍬 **HABITAT** *United States*

🍬 **DESCRIPTION** *These rosettes feature an orange flavor that yields a Creamsicle-like candy. The ingredients make a creamy-textured candy that is piped out of a pastry bag with a star-shaped tip.*

🍬 **FIELD NOTES** *You could certainly use other citrus flavorings such as lemon, tangerine, or lime oil. I like Boyajian citrus oils, available at Whole Foods stores nationwide or through Williams-Sonoma. Note that these candies need to dry for two overnight periods.*

🍬 **LIFESPAN** *2 weeks at room temperature in airtight container in single layers separated by waxed or parchment paper*

Yield: *about 100 rosettes*

Tools: *Pastry bag fitted with a large star-shaped tip, such as Ateco #823*

▷●◁ INGREDIENTS

4 to 5 cups confectioners' sugar
3 ounces cream cheese, at room
  temperature, cut into pieces
2 teaspoons heavy cream or evaporated
  milk

$^1/_4$ teaspoon orange oil
Red and yellow liquid food coloring
  (optional)

▷●◁ DIRECTIONS

1. Line a jelly-roll pan with aluminum foil, smoothing out any wrinkles.

2. In a large bowl with an electric mixer on medium speed, beat 4 cups confectioners' sugar, cream cheese, heavy cream, and orange oil until thick and creamy, about 3 minutes. The mixture should be creamy, smooth, and stiff enough to hold peaks, but not too stiff to pipe out of a pastry bag. Add more confectioners' sugar as necessary. Add a drop or two of yellow and red food coloring, if desired, to make a pale orange color.

3. Scrape mixture into a pastry bag fitted with a star tip. Pipe out small rosettes onto prepared pan, spaced apart so they don't touch. Allow to air-dry overnight, uncovered. Remove with spatula to a cooling rack and allow undersides to dry completely; usually another overnight period will do it.

Candy Tidbits

To embellish these even further, you could put a tiny piece of candied orange peel on the top center of each rosette while the mixture is still soft, as in the photo.

Sesame Honey Candies
(Melekouni)

🍬 **HOLIDAY** *Weddings*

🍬 **TYPE** *Poured candy*   🍬 **HABITAT** *Greece*

🍬 **DESCRIPTION** *This simple candy has two ingredients—honey and sesame seeds. It is sweet and chewy. Sometimes, as in the photo above, the candies are embellished with almonds—okay, make that three ingredients.*

🍬 **FIELD NOTES** *This candy is offered at Greek weddings and it is meant to herald a sweet life and many children for the betrothed. Be sure to use hulled sesame seeds; they are a more delicate color and more tender than unhulled.*

🍬 **LIFESPAN** *2 weeks at room temperature in airtight container*

Yield: *40 diamonds*

INGREDIENTS

1 1/2 cups hulled sesame seeds
1 cup honey
20 blanched whole almonds (optional)

40 small square candy wrappers or
cellophane

DIRECTIONS

1. Preheat oven to 350°F. Scatter seeds in a single layer on a jelly-roll pan. Bake for about 7 minutes, stirring often, until light golden brown. Place seeds in a small bowl. Allow pan to cool, wipe clean, and brush with canola oil.

2. Bring honey to a boil in a medium saucepan over medium heat. Simmer for 1 minute, or until foamy. Stir in seeds and simmer for 4 minutes on low heat, stirring frequently. The mixture will be golden in color. Immediately scrape mixture onto prepared pan and spread thinly with an offset spatula, to about 1/3-inch thickness. Don't worry too much about the shape of the mass; the thickness is what is important. Let cool briefly, then score into diamond shapes with a knife. While the candy is still warm, carefully split almonds lengthwise and place one almond half, flat side down, in the center of each candy, if desired.

3. Let mixture sit until cooled and set. Cut into diamond shapes with a sharp knife dipped in water to help prevent sticking. Wrap individually in candy wrappers.

Candy Tidbits

You can try using a wooden board rinsed with water instead of the oiled pan. Refer to Honey Walnut Candies (page 24) for directions.

Resources

Australian Catalogue Company
146 Riverview Park Drive
Jackson, Georgia 30233
(800) 808-0938
(770) 775-2244
www.aussiecatalog.com
Sells the copha called for in the Australian White Christmas candies, as well as other Australian foods.

Beryl's Cake Decorating and Pastry Supplies
P.O. Box 1584
North Springfield, VA 22151
(703) 256-6951
(800) 488-2749
FAX (703) 750-3779
www.beryls.com
There is a Beryl, who will often answer the phone herself. This is one of my first stops for bakery supplies. She provides highly personal and professional customer service and her company supplies chocolates, decorating tips, Boyajian oils, gold and silver leaf, books, and more.

Blue Magic
The Luce Corporation
336 Putnam Avenue
P.O. Box 4124
Hamden, CT 06514
(203) 787-0281
Blue Magic moisture absorbers are small devices a little larger than a walnut that have a clear glass bottom and perforated metal top. Inside is a dry chemical that absorbs moisture. You place one of these devices in your candy jar and it absorbs any excess moisture. It's called "blue" magic because the chemical changes from blue to pinkish-white as it absorbs moisture. When it has completely turned pinkish-white, you just dry it out in the oven or toaster oven, and when it's blue again, it's ready to use once more. You can buy the small units by themselves to place in your

own containers, or you can buy canisters that have the Blue Magic unit built in.

Cape Cod Provisions
55 Jonathan Bourne Drive
Pocasset, MA 02559
(888) 811-2379
This company will mail you 6-ounce retail packs of the moistest, most delicious dried cranberries you have ever tasted. Just ask for the Paradise Meadow cranberries.

The Chef's Catalog
3215 Commercial Avenue
Northbrook, IL 60062-1900
(800) 338-3232
www.chefscatalog.com
This is a great mail-order catalog with very competitive prices. You'll find KitchenAid mixers, large professional-size rubber spatulas, extra-long hot mitts, parchment paper, and more.

Chocosphere
(877) 99CHOCO
FAX (877) 992-4626
www.chocosphere.com
If you are looking for high-quality chocolate, make this your first stop. This company specializes in all my favorite chocolates that are great both to eat and to use in your candies. Owners Jerry and Joanne Kryszek offer excellent personal service, and they ship nationwide.

ChocoVision
(800) 324-6252
sales@chocovision.com
www.chocovision.com
This company sells some molds and features a few recipes and tools, but is known for its home-size chocolate tempering machine. For about $350 you can have a temperer that will automatically temper white, milk, and dark chocolates for all your candy needs. I have had mine for years and love it.

King Arthur Flour
The Baker's Catalogue
P.O. Box 876
Norwich, VT 05055
(800) 827-6836
FAX (802) 649-5359
www.kingarthurflour.com
Offers high-quality extracts, chocolates, candied fruit and citrus rinds, scales, and high-quality measuring cups, including ones in odd sizes. They have small ice cream scoops that make scooping candy mixtures quick and easy; ask for the Zeroll brand in the "teaspoon" and "tablespoon" sizes. The #100 size corresponds to a generous teaspoon, and the #40 size dishes up a generous tablespoon. Order American Almond almond paste from them too.

KitchenAid
P.O. Box 218
St. Joseph, MI 49085
(800) 541-6390
www.kitchenaid.com
Go directly to this Web site for a complete listing of their high-quality products. All of my candies were tested with a KitchenAid stove and made with a KitchenAid mixer. I bought my mixer almost 20 years ago and it is still going strong—this is a worthwhile investment for any avid cook.

Kitchen Krafts
P.O. Box 442
Waukon, IA 52172
(800) 776-0575
FAX (800) 850-3093
www.kitchenkrafts.com
This company carries everything from KitchenAid mixers to small tools. They also have a special candy maker's catalog. They sell my favorite digital thermometer, the 3-D sucker mold used with the cinnamon candies, coloring,

chocolate dipping tools, chocolate tempering machines, citric acid, lollipop sticks, candy wrappers, rubber maple-leaf molds, and much more.

LorAnn Oils
P.O. Box 22009
Lansing, MI 48909
(517) 882-0215
(888) 4-LORANN
FAX (517) 882-0507
www.lorannoils.com
This company has many items a candy maker needs, such as flavorings (both extracts and oils), molds, candy bags, twist ties, foil wrappers, lollipop sticks, and coloring. They even have a sugar-free candy-making kit. You can often find their products at craft stores and stores carrying cake decorating and candy-making ingredients and equipment.

Maverick Industries, Inc.
94 Mayfield Avenue
Edison, NJ 08837
800-526-0954
(732) 417-9666
FAX (732) 417-9673
info@maverickhousewares.com
www.maverickhousewares.com
For the recipes in this book, you will need an accurate thermometer that has the proper range of temperatures used in candy making. And you might as well have one that is easy to use! I use the Maverick CT-03 Redi Chek Digital Thermometer and absolutely love it. It has an 8-inch-long probe with an easy-to-position clip, so you can adjust it for any height pot. The display is easy to read and it even features pre-programmed settings and can alert you with loud audible beeps when your foods reach the proper temperature. It's also easy to clean and comes with batteries.

New York Cake and Baking Distributors
56 West 22nd Street
New York, NY 10010
(212) 675-2253
(800) 942-2539
www.nycakesupplies.com
You can shop here for food colors, colored sugars, jelly-roll pans, parchment paper, high-quality chocolates, and more.

Penzeys Spices
P.O. Box 993
W19362 Apollo Drive
Muskego, WI 53150
(800) 741-7787
www.penzeys.com
This company has an amazing array of fresh herbs and spices. Check them out for excellent cinnamon, nutmeg, ginger, and vanilla extract, among other ingredients.

Reign Trading Company
3838 Walnut Grove
Rosemead, CA 91770
(626) 307-7755
FAX (626) 307-7744
www.mexicansugarskull.com
This company offers all sorts of products associated with the Mexican holiday of the Day of the Dead. I used their Original Medium Mold with a flat back for my candy skulls. They also have meringue powder, colors, etc. Retail locations listed on the Web site, or you can fax or e-mail an order.

Sur La Table
Pike Place Farmers Market
84 Pine Street
Seattle, WA 98101
(206) 448-2244
(800) 243-0852
www.surlatable.com
Here you will find high-quality jelly-roll pans, high-heat spatulas, great measuring cups, and more. If you can visit one of their stores, you will find dozens of gorgeous platters and dishes for serving your candy.

Sweet Celebrations
7009 Washington Avenue South
Edina, MN 55439
(800) 328-6722
www.sweetc.com
www.maidofscandinavia.com
This company used to be called Maid of Scandinavia, but is now called Sweet Celebrations. They offer a huge array of equipment and ingredients, such as great chocolates, candy flavorings, paper candy wrappers and boxes, molds, lollipop sticks, and more.

Tomric Plastics, Inc.
85 River Rock Drive, Suite 202
Buffalo, NY 14207
(716) 854-6050
FAX (716) 854-0081
www.tomric.com
If you are looking for chocolate and candy molds, make sure to check out this company's catalog. They'll have the shape you want, from Easter bunnies and eggs to hearts, pigs, shells, fish, soccer balls, and trains. Great customer service too.

Williams-Sonoma
P.O. Box 7456
San Francisco, CA 94120
(415) 421-4242
(800) 541-2233
FAX (415) 421-5253
www.williams-sonoma.com
Sells well-made accurate measuring tools, KitchenAid mixers, vanilla extract, some chocolate and cocoa, and other baking equipment, including jelly-roll pans and spatulas of all sorts.

Wilton Industries, Inc.
2240 West 75th Street
Woodbridge, IL 60517
(708) 963-7100
(800) 794-5866
www.wilton.com
Great catalog with food colors, food-safe markers, parchment paper, chocolates, cocoa, molds (I love their Easter egg mold), lollipop sticks, and much more.

Measurement Equivalents

Please note that all conversions are approximate.

Liquid Conversions

U.S.	Metric
1 tsp	5 ml
1 tbs	15 ml
2 tbs	30 ml
3 tbs	45 ml
¼ cup	60 ml
⅓ cup	75 ml
⅓ cup + 1 tbs	90 ml
⅓ cup + 2 tbs	100 ml
½ cup	120 ml
⅔ cup	150 ml
¾ cup	180 ml
¾ cup + 2 tbs	200 ml
1 cup	240 ml
1 cup + 2 tbs	275 ml
1¼ cups	300 ml
1⅓ cups	325 ml
1½ cups	350 ml
1⅔ cups	375 ml
1¾ cups	400 ml
1¾ cups + 2 tbs	450 ml
2 cups (1 pint)	475 ml
2½ cups	600 ml
3 cups	720 ml
4 cups (1 quart)	945 ml (1,000 ml is 1 liter)

Weight Conversions

U.S./U.K.	Metric
½ oz	14 g
1 oz	28 g
1½ oz	43 g
2 oz	57 g
2½ oz	71 g
3 oz	85 g
3½ oz	100 g
4 oz	113 g
5 oz	142 g
6 oz	170 g
7 oz	200 g
8 oz	227 g
9 oz	255 g
10 oz	284 g
11 oz	312 g
12 oz	340 g
13 oz	368 g
14 oz	400 g
15 oz	425 g
1 lb	454 g

Oven Temperature Conversions

°F	Gas Mark	°C
250	½	120
275	1	140
300	2	150
325	3	165
350	4	180
375	5	190
400	6	200
425	7	220
450	8	230
475	9	240
500	10	260
550	Broil	290

Index